R3

Co

Software and architecture

Computer Systems: Software and architecture

John L. Newman MSc BSc

Senior Lecturer in Computer Studies, North-East Wales Institute of Further and Higher Education

Hutchinson

London   Melbourne   Sydney   Auckland   Johannesburg

Hutchinson Education

An imprint of Century Hutchinson Limited

62–65 Chandos Place, London WC2N 4NW

Century Hutchinson Group (Australia) Pty Ltd
16–22 Church Street, Hawthorn, Melbourne, Victoria 3122

Century Hutchinson Group (NZ) Ltd
32–34 View Road, PO Box 40–086, Glenfield, Auckland 10

Century Hutchinson Group (SA) (Pty) Ltd
PO Box 337, Bergvlei 2012, South Africa

First published 1986

Set in Plantin by Activity Ltd, Salisbury, Wilts

Printed and bound in Great Britain by
Anchor Brendon Ltd, Tiptree, Essex

British Library Cataloguing in Publication Data

Newman, John L.
   Computer systems: software and architecture.—
   (Hutchinson computer studies series)
   1. Computer programs
   I. Title
   005.3   QA76.6

ISBN 0–09–159451–0

To Micki,
Jeremy Paul, Joel
and Laura

Contents

Editor's note

This book is one of a series of textbooks with a modular structure aimed at students of computer studies and designed for use on courses at most levels of academic and professional qualification. A coherent approach to the development of courses in computing has emerged over the last few years with the introduction of the BTEC National, Higher National and Post-Experience Awards in Computer Studies. The syllabus guidelines for these courses have provided the focus for this series of books, and this ensures that the books are relevant to a wide range of courses at intermediate level.

Many existing books on computing cause frustration to teachers and students because, in trying to be all embracing, they usually include irrelevant material and fail to tackle relevant material in adequate depth. The books in this series are specific in their treatment of topics and practical in their orientation. They provide a firm foundation in all the key areas of computer studies, which are seen as: computer technology; programming the computer; analysing and designing computer-based systems; and applications of the computer.

There are sixteen books in the series.

Computer Appreciation and BASIC Programming is the introductory book. It is intended to put the computer into context both for the layman who wants to understand a little more about computers and their usage, and for the student as a background for further study.

Computing in a Small Business is aimed specifically at the small businessman, or at the student who will be working in a small business, and sets out to provide a practical guide to implementing computer-based systems in a small business. It is a comprehensive treatment of most aspects of computing.

Fundamentals of Computing looks in considerably more depth than the previous two books at the basic concepts of the technology. Its major emphasis is on hardware, with an introduction to

system software. *Computer Systems: Software and architecture* develops from this base and concentrates on software, especially operating systems, language processors and data base management systems; it concludes with a section on networks. *Computer Hardware and Industrial Control* aims to provide a fairly complete description and understanding of a general microprocessor-based system with an emphasis on industrial/control applications.

An Introduction to Program Design is about how to design computer programs based on the Michael Jackson method. Examples of program code are given in BASIC, Pascal and COBOL, but this is not a book about a programming language since there are plenty of these books already available. This title complements *Program Development: Tools and techniques*, which looks at the task of programming from all angles and is independent of program design methods, programming languages and machines. *Scientific Programming* aims to give a broad and practical view of scientific computing, developing necessary concepts while also revealing some of the problems inherent in solution by computer.

Data Processing Methods provides a fairly detailed treatment of the methods which lie behind computer-based systems in terms of modes of processing, input and output of data, storage of data, and security of systems. Several applications are described. *Information Systems* follows it up by looking at the role of data processing in organizations. This book deals with organizations and their information systems as systems, and with how information systems contribute to and affect the functioning of an organization. *Decision Support Systems* is concerned with the use of computers, in particular microcomputers, by management for decision making; it examines the hardware/software aspects, approaches to building such systems, and a number of examples.

Basic Systems Analysis offers an introduction to

the knowledge and skills required by a systems analyst, with rather more emphasis on feasibility, investigation, implementation and review than on design. *Basic Systems Design*, the related volume, tackles design in considerable depth and looks at current methods of structured systems design. *Management of System Development* aims to give the reader the skills to plan and monitor system development projects as well as an understanding of the policy-making and strategic planning required in information systems development. *Formal Methods of Systems Analysis and Design* rounds off these books by taking a historical perspective of the development of formal methods over the last twenty years, with detailed discus-

sion of automation and of the latest thinking.

Case Exercises in Computing is the final book in the series at the moment, and provides a large number of case studies with questions to provide practical work in most areas of computing work. The exercises are all based on real life, and suggested solutions are available separately to bona fide teachers.

The books in this series stand alone, but all are related to each other so that duplication is avoided.

Barry S. Lee
Series editor

Preface

This book is intended to meet the needs of students taking a first course in operating systems, language processors, database management systems or computer networks.

The first section of the book covers operating systems and language processors. Chapter 1 deals with the historical development of operating systems from the early manual systems to the modern operating systems. The user's view of an operating system depends upon the manner in which he/she expresses his/her requirements. The ways in which a user can express the job control are covered in Chapter 2. Much of the material within this section is devoted to the management of resources in a multiprogramming operating system. The scheduling of processor time, the management of main store and backing storage space and the management of peripherals are covered in some detail. The nature of programming languages is changing from the traditional procedural languages to a non-procedural approach to programming. However, many of the techniques for translating programs into machine code remain the same. The stages involved in translating a program from source code into object code are described in Chapter 5.

The second section of the book is on databases. Chapter 6 describes the architecture of a database management system. The difference between the external, conceptual and physical views of a database are explained. The different database approaches are distinguished by the way in which the data is represented. The method of representing and accessing data for each of the three most common approaches – relational, hierarchical and network are described in Chapter 7.

The third section of the book covers computer networks. The principles of data transmission between two devices are covered in Chapter 8. Chapter 9 deals with the necessity for agreed network protocols and the ISO standards for these protocols. Algorithms for routing data through various networks are described in some detail. The final chapter is concerned with local area networks in particular Ethernet and Cambridge **Ring networks**.

The structure of a typical modern computer system is shown in the diagram below:

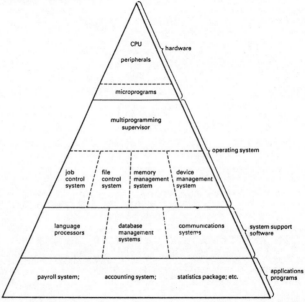

Acknowledgements

I would like to thank Barry Lee for suggesting that I should write this book. Thanks also to my family who have suffered during the many hours that it has taken to write it. My wife, Micki, in particular has spent hours reading draft material and correcting my mistakes. I would like to thank Dr Barry Eaglestone and Dr Ian Bradley for their constructive comments on the content. I would also like to offer special thanks to Debbie Moses who typed the manuscript.

Part One

Systems software

1 The development of operating systems

This chapter traces the development of operating systems software from the very earliest computer systems to those in use today. The evolution of the operating system is closely related to that of hardware developments. An operating system is designed to make optimum use of the available hardware and to provide, through software, facilities not provided by the hardware.

The operating system has, through the years, taken on an increasing role, providing more and more facilities for the user. The developments in operating system design have always been made with the intention of optimizing the utilization of the hardware and providing a simpler interface with which the user can work.

The very earliest computing machines were constructed without any software at all. The computer users were usually highly skilled mathematicians who performed the functions of both programmer and operator. Significant among the early computers were ENIAC (Electronic Numerical Integrator and Calculator), completed in 1946, which was programmed using plugboards and worked in decimal, and the ASCC (Automatic Sequence Control Calculator), which executed programs held on paper tape and also worked in decimal. Today it is difficult to envisage that a program's instructions should be held anywhere except in the computer's memory, but on these very early machines the programs were held on external media. The stored program concept was first proposed publicly in a draft report by Dr John Von Neumann in 1945 in which he proposed a new computer, EDVAC (Electronic Discrete Variable Computer), which incorporated a stored program facility. (Also proposed in Von Neumann's report was the use of the binary number system for the internal representation of information, and since 1950 all computers have made use of the binary representation.) The first machine to execute a stored program was EDSAC (Electronic Delay Storage Automatic Calculator) in May 1949. EDSAC was built at Cambridge University by a team led by Professor Maurice Wilkes. This development led to the first item of system software, the bootstrap loader.

Bootstrap loaders

When a computer is switched on, its memory is initially empty. The operating system must be loaded into part of this empty store. The bootstrap loader is responsible for loading the operating system, which in turn is responsible for loading subsequent programs.

On the earliest machines, which predate operating systems, the bootstrap loader was responsible for loading each program. The loading sequence would be typically

1 The operator would key in an initial sequence of instructions, sufficient to read in one or two punched cards containing the binary image of a basic program loader.
2 The punched cards containing the basic program loader were placed in front of the deck of cards containing the program. When the program loader had been read, it would control the reading of the deck of cards that followed.

A common approach on modern systems is to build the initial load sequence into the processor. The sequence will be entered directly when the operator switches on the computer. The initial load sequence will read a more sophisticated loader, with built-in error checking facilities, from a systems disk. This more sophisticated loader will load the rest of the operating system. The operating system then controls the loading of programs.

Hardware developments

It is not the intention of this book to provide a full history of hardware developments, but certain of these have had a profound effect upon the design of operating systems and are described below.

Channel processors

Prior to the introduction of the IBM 709 in 1958, all peripheral transfers were treated in the same way as other instructions. The processor would initiate the execution of the instruction and then control its execution. This meant that the processor was unable to process further instructions until the transfer had been completed. Input/output transfers have always taken much longer than, for example, arithmetic instructions. Many of these input/output transfers were to slow peripherals, which meant that the processor was idle for a large part of the time (see Figure 1).

The concept of the channel processor was introduced on the IBM 709. This separated the control of input/output instructions from the control of other instructions (Figure 2). The processing is shared between the channel processor and the central processor. The execution of peripheral transfer instructions is controlled by the channel processors, while the execution of other instructions is controlled by the central processor. When the central processor detects an input or an output instruction it passes all the information necessary for the execution of the instruction to the appropriate channel processor. Once the channel processor has been informed of the device referred to, the direction and mode of transfer, the address of the storage locations involved and the amount of data to be transferred,

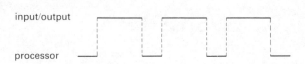

Figure 1   *Timing diagram for part of a program's execution*

the central processor is free to fetch another instruction for execution. For the duration of the data transfer, the area of store required will be locked out to the central processor (see 'Storage lockout' in Chapter 3). The channel processor will inform the central processor of any errors that occur during the execution of the instruction.

The effect of channel processors upon the performance of a computer can be illustrated by considering the following sequence of instructions:

    10 INPUT X
    20 LET Y = Y + 1
    30 LET X = X + 1

The input instruction will be passed to the channel processor for execution, leaving the central processor free to execute the instructions following. The third instruction, however, cannot be obeyed until the input instruction has terminated (see Figure 3).

Interrupts

In the example above, when the central processor attempts to access the location X it will find that the location has been locked out. The central processor could repeatedly attempt to access the

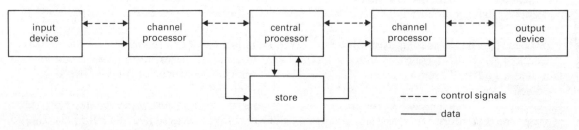

Figure 2   *Channel processor usage*

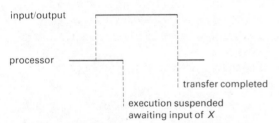

input/output

processor

transfer completed

execution suspended
awaiting input of *X*

Figure 3   *Timing diagram showing execution of instruction sequence 10–30 in text*

contents of location X until the peripheral transfer is completed, but this makes inefficient use of the central processor. It is better for the channel processor to inform the central processor that the transfer has been completed, thus releasing the central processor to perform other tasks. The signal from the channel processor informing the central processor that the transfer has finished is called an interrupt. The first documented application of interrupts used to signal the completion of a peripheral transfer is on the UNIVAC 1103.

Interrupt signals are now used to indicate to the operating system that any one of a variety of events has occurred, such as

1. Machine failure, e.g. power loss or main memory parity error
2. Clock pulse, used to indicate time intervals in a multi-access system
3. Peripheral transfer completed
4. Peripheral transfer exception condition (e.g. printer out of paper or magnetic tape parity error)
5. Attempt to access a program address that is not resident in main memory or which may not be accessed by this program
6. Command from operator's console
7. Program termination
8. Instruction error, e.g. an attempt to divide by zero.

An interrupt is a signal that may be generated by hardware or software and indicates a change in the state of the processor or process that generated the signal.

When an interrupt occurs, the interrupt handling routine must determine the cause of the interrupt and call the appropriate interrupt service routine.

Determining the cause of an interrupt

The simplest method for determining the cause of an interrupt is to have a single interrupt request line that is shared by all devices likely to cause an interrupt. To interrupt the CPU a device sends a signal along the interrupt request line. The CPU will complete the instruction currently being executed and then poll each of the devices in turn to determine the source of the interrupt. This system, however, presumes that there is only one reason for each device to interrupt.

A slightly faster way to determine the cause of an interrupt is to have multiple interrupt request lines. Each device will generate an interrupt signal on its own interrupt request line; consequently the source of the interrupt is known immediately. A variation of this is to associate a separate interrupt request line with each possible type of interrupt condition. Each interrupt request line will be associated with a flag. These flags may be held collectively in an interrupt register. When an interrupt occurs the appropriate register bit is set. The interrupt handling routine examines each bit in turn and, when a bit is found to be set, branches to the appropriate interrupt service routine. The bits set by the more commonly occurring interrupt conditions will be examined first. If there are a large number of possible interrupt conditions, then determining the cause of the interrupt can be a time-consuming process. The process can be speeded up by allowing each bit of the interrupt register to indicate a group of interrupt conditions. The actual cause of the interrupt is indicated by a second level of interrupt registers.

The fastest method of determining the cause of an interrupt is for each possible interrupt condition to generate a memory address. This address can lead directly to the appropriate interrupt service routine. The address may be generated in a number of ways. If there is a single interrupt request line then the device generating the interrupt will transmit an interrupt signal. The CPU responds with an interrupt acknowledgement signal. The acknowledgement signal will be received by each device in turn. When the device that generated the interrupt signal receives the acknowledgement it will place the memory address on the address lines of the system highway. If there are multiple interrupt request lines then each line can be used to generate a different memory address. The term *vectored interrupts* is usually used to describe the technique of transferring control directly to the interrupt service routine by supplying the start address of the service routine to the CPU. The address transmitted could be the start address of the appropriate interrupt service routine. However, this restricts the system to having fixed start addresses for all interrupt service routines.

It is preferable that the address transmitted by the device is used either as an index to a table of interrupt service routine addresses or to point to a memory location that contains the address of the interrupt service routine. The program that is running must have its program counter and register values stored. These values may be stored in specific memory locations, such as location O for the program counter, but as interrupt calls may be nested (i.e. a second interrupt occurs during the processing of the first) this value may be overwritten. The program counter and register values may be placed upon a stack, then when the processing of an interrupt is complete the CPU returns to processing the task that was being run when the interrupt occurred. Alternatively the program counter and register values may be placed in storage locations belonging to the task being interrupted.

When the program counter value has been stored then the address of the interrupt service routine can be placed in the program counter. The first instruction of the interrupt service routine can now be executed.

The sequence of events can be summarized as

1   A device generates an interrupt signal.
2   The CPU completes execution of the current instruction and transmits an acknowledgement signal.
3   In a single interrupt request line system, the device will then transmit a memory address. In a multiple interrupt request line system, the memory address will be generated.
4   The current program counter and register values are stored.

5   The contents of the memory location identified by the memory address are loaded into the program counter.
6   The first instruction of the interrupt service routine is executed.

Handling an interrupt

When an interrupt occurs, the instruction currently being executed will usually be completed before the interrupt handling routine is entered. The exception to this is when the cause of the interrupt prevents the execution of the instruction being completed, such as an attempt to access a program location that is not currently in main store.

The current processing state of the program that is interrupted must be preserved. One technique is to store the current values of the program counter and other program registers. Alternatively, a completely separate set of registers can be used by the interrupt system.

At certain times during the processing of an interrupt, such as when the contents of the program registers are being preserved, no other interrupts should be allowed. During these periods, the interrupt mechanism should be disabled. In a simple interrupt handling system, the interrupt mechanism is disabled when an interrupt occurs and enabled again when the interrupt has been processed. Any interrupts that occur during this period will be queued until the interrupt mechanism is enabled.

More sophisticated interrupt systems allow an interrupt service routine to be interrupted, but only by a more significant interrupt condition. There are two ways in which this type of interrupt system can be organized. The first approach is for the processor to have multiple levels of interrupt service routines. Each level has its own set of registers so that when an interrupt occurs the register values of the routine being interrupted do not have to be saved. Each interrupt condition is associated with a particular level. When an interrupt occurs it will be ignored if it is at a lower level. An interrupt service routine can only be interrupted by an interrupt occurring at a higher level.

The second approach is to use an interrupt mask register. Each bit of the interrupt mask register represents one possible interrupt condition. If the register bit is set then the interrupt condition is disabled. This mechanism allows each interrupt service routine to selectively disable other possible interrupt conditions.

Magnetic core storage
The significance of magnetic core storage to operating systems design is that it was the first cheap reliable storage technology to be available in relatively large storage modules. Until the advent of core store, memories were only large enough to hold a single program. Magnetic core store memories were the first to be constructed large enough to hold a multiprogramming control program and two or more user programs. With two or more programs in store at the same time it became necessary to introduce a system of memory protection (see Chapter 3).

Virtual memory
It is possible to create the illusion that the usable memory space is actually larger than the physical memory. The addressable memory space is defined by the number of bits used to represent each address. For example, a twenty-four-bit address gives access to 16M locations. The physical memory size may be much smaller. Mapping the addressable memory space on to the physical memory is achieved by the memory management system loading only part of each program at a time. If the addressable memory available to the user is larger than the physical memory then it is known as a virtual memory.

Virtual memory systems make it possible to increase the level of multiprogramming.

Privileged instructions set
The operating system must be able to perform certain functions denied to the ordinary user. In a multiprogramming environment it must be able to start and stop programs and must be able to read or write directly to peripherals. In order to achieve this, the operating system must have a set of privileged instructions.

To ensure that privileged instructions can only be executed by the operating system the computer system will have two different modes of operation: a user mode and a supervisor mode. Only when the mode bit is set to indicate supervisor mode can these instructions be obeyed.

Fast peripherals
The first magnetic surface recording device, the magnetic drum, was introduced not as a backing store but as a main memory. The first magnetic tape stores were introduced in the early 1950s and the first magnetic disk stores were introduced in the latter half of that decade, although neither became popular until the 1960s. Magnetic tapes and disks were introduced as fast peripheral storage devices.

Magnetic surface recording devices transfer data much faster than the slower mechanical devices such as card readers and printers. The processing capabilities of a monoprogramming computer system could be improved by transferring all input and output data to or from magnetic tape off-line.

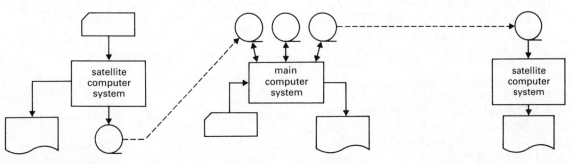

Figure 4   *Off-lining*

Consider the timing diagram for a computer system equipped with channel processors (Figure 3). From the point at which the program is suspended, execution of the program cannot continue until the data areas involved in the peripheral transfer are released. If the time taken to transfer the data can be reduced, then the central processor may resume processing other instructions sooner. The only way of reducing the length of time for which the central processor is idle is to use faster peripherals.

In the late 1950s computer systems were constructed which used the technique of *off-lining* to speed up processing (Figure 4). The raw input data on punched cards would be transferred to magnetic tape by a small satellite processor. The operator could then transfer the magnetic tape to the main computer system where the program, also loaded from magnetic tape, would be run. Most of the output produced by the program would be directed to a magnetic tape on which it would be held until it could be printed by a separate satellite processor.

The input satellite computer system would produce control information on the operator's console, indicating the contents of the tape but not the actual data values.

A card reader attached to the main computer system would be used to input job control cards (see Chapter 2). Error conditions and small volumes of data would be printed on the printer or operator's console of the main computer system.

Off-lining using magnetic tapes gave way to systems using fixed disks which could be shared by both the main computer system and the small satellite systems, thus reducing the necessity to transfer tapes between computers.

The technique of off-lining led to the development of two further techniques. The first of these took the input satellite processor out of the computer room and into the data preparation room where it was used for key-to-tape and key-to-disk data preparation. The second occurred with the advent of multiprogramming systems; the transfer of data from slow peripherals to fast backing storage devices could be performed as a background process on-line called *spooling* (Simultaneous Peripheral Operating On-Line).

In order that off-lining and spooling could remain invisible to the user, all input and output had to be performed using library subroutines. Compilers for high-level languages, such as FORTRAN, could automatically incorporate subroutine calls to the input and output routines in the object version of a program. Writers of assembler language programs were still free to handle peripherals directly. However, this led to programmers inadvertently reading past the end of file markers and reading other users' programs or data. To avoid this, the responsibility for all input and output was transferred to the control of an input/output management system (see Chapter 3).

Buffering

In order to make the best possible use of channel processors, the programming technique of double buffering was developed (Figure 5). This involves reading a new record into a second buffer while processing the record that has already been read into the first buffer. By the time the new record has been read in, the processing of the first buffer should have been completed and the roles of the buffers can be reversed. A new record can now be read into the first buffer while the contents of second buffer are processed.

Most data is spooled on to a fast backing storage device before being input to a program. The transfer of data between the backing storage device and the store is performed by transferring blocks of data. The amount of data read by a READ instruction in a program may be a single character, a numeric value or a record; as a consequence, not every program READ instruction results in a physical transfer of data between the peripheral device and the store. Double

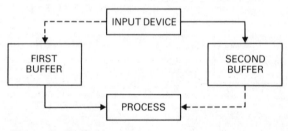

Figure 5   *Buffering*

buffering is only applicable to the physical transfer of data and is not applicable to the logical READ instructions.

The storage areas reserved for the buffers should not occupy contiguous memory locations as this may result in both buffers being locked out as the same time.

Parallelism
The fall in the cost of hardware has led to an increase in parallel processing. This is evident in a number of ways.

Pipelining
The execution of an instruction can be considered as a number of distinct stages (Figure 6). These stages – instruction fetch, instruction decode, address calculation, data fetch, instruction execution, storage of result and incrementing the program counter – are usually summarized as the fetch–execute cycle. They can, however, be considered as distinct stages, the execution of which can be allowed to overlap. The overlapping of the stages of instruction execution is shown as pipelining.

The timing of each stage must be carefully controlled. This can be achieved under clock control, which means that the time taken to execute each stage will be the same. The time must be equivalent to the length of time necessary to execute the slowest stage. Alternatively, each stage must have an agreed synchronization protocol with the succeeding and preceding stages.

Conditional branch instructions can cause problems. When a conditional branch instruction is encountered, the path to be taken must be predicted. The prediction can be based upon the assumption that the result of a condition test will always be false, or on the assumption that the result of a condition test will be the same on successive passes through the code.

Functional parallelism
The processor may have several independent functional units, each responsible for the execution of a separate function. For example, there may be separate units for multiplication, division, fixed-point addition and subtraction, floating-point addition and subtraction, and logical operations. The execution of instructions can take place in parallel providing that the appropriate functional units are free. The time taken to execute instructions varies and the instructions may not be completed in the same sequence in which they are fetched. This can cause problems when an interrupt occurs as the instruction causing the interrupt may have been executed prior to instructions that were fetched earlier. The execution of an instruction may be delayed because the instruction is dependent upon operands or functional units still required by previous instructions.

Array processors
The execution of a program frequently involves processing the elements of an array. On a conventional machine the array elements are processed one at a time. An array processor is designed to process each of the elements of the array in parallel. An array processor is a special processor with an array of functional execution units. There is only one instruction fetch and decode unit. When an instruction applicable to an array of data items is fetched and decoded then the operation may be applied to every element of the array in parallel.

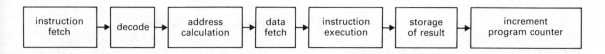

Figure 6   *Pipelining*

Operating systems developments

Manual systems

The earliest computer systems had no operating software. The method of operation was entirely manual; every stage of processing a job required operator intervention. The amount of storage space available was only sufficient for a single program. Both the source and object versions of the program were held on an external medium such as punched cards or paper tape. A typical run to compile and execute a program would be

1   Load the binary version of the compiler. Typically this would be held on punched cards as these were more durable than paper tape. The compiler usually required more than one pass (see Chapter 5), so each pass would need to be loaded separately.
2   Load the source version of the program to be compiled. This would probably be held on paper tape as tape was a more popular input medium on the early computers. (The first pass of the compiler would produce an internal representation of the program also on paper tape which would be the input to the second pass of the compiler.)
3   Load the binary version of the second pass of the compiler.
4   Load the paper tape produced by the first pass of the compiler. (This process would be repeated for each pass until the final object version of the program was produced.)
5   Load the object version of the program.
6   Load subroutines. (Standard subroutines would be held as object versions on punched cards; the operator would select the required subroutines and load these into the card reader.)
7   Load data, which would be on paper tape. (The output from the program would also be produced on paper tape and printed off-line at a terminal.)

Although the sequence of steps above would be controlled by an operator, the programmer was usually present. During the running of the program, status lights on the computer console would inform the programmer what was happening during the execution of his program.

Job processors

The forerunner of the operating system was the control program. The first control programs were introduced in the latter part of the 1950s. These simple control systems automated the steps of running a job.

The advent of magnetic tapes and disks meant that the object versions of compilers, user programs and library subroutines could now be held on backing storage devices. Magnetic tapes were more popular than magnetic disks until the middle of the 1960s.

Control cards would be used to identify the compiler required. The loader would search the magnetic tape to find the object version of the compiler. When the program had been compiled, the linkage editor would be used to search the tape file in order to locate the subroutines called by the user's program.

The early magnetic tape- and disk-based systems used off-lining techniques to speed up processing. A complete job would be set up and control statements, programs and data would be transferred to a magnetic tape or disk off-line. The control program would process each job in turn. The output from each program would be directed to a magnetic tape and printed off-line.

Early multiprogramming systems

The first multiprogramming systems appeared in the early 1960s. These systems were limited to running two or three programs at a time. One of the reasons for this limitation was the size of the main store. A typical main store memory would have 32K words of store. Part of the store would hold the resident supervisory routine and the rest of the storage space would be available for user programs.

The computer system was usually divided into streams. Each stream was assigned a portion of the system's resources. This allocation could be changed by loading a different version of the supervisory routine. The operator would select the stream in which a job would be run. The user would specify his requirements to the operator on a job submission document, from which the operator would interpret the user's requirements.

Early operating systems
There has been a continual expansion of computer memory size and processor power since the early days of computing, which is still continuing. As the memory size and processing power increases, so does the number of programs that can be multiprogrammed. By the late 1960s the level of multiprogramming had increased to the point where several programs could be run simultaneously. The sharing of resources between a greater number of programs meant that routines to control the allocation of resources became necessary. It was no longer sufficient to divide the computer system into streams with a fixed allocation of resources to each stream. Resources had to be allocated dynamically to each program. The resources to be considered for allocation included processor time, main storage space, file storage space, channels and peripherals.

The first experimental multi-access systems were developed in the early 1960s and by the late 1960s they had become generally available. The first experimental systems handled very few terminals, but as the level of multiprogramming increased so did the number of terminals that could be handled. Multi-access systems placed different demands upon the operating system. One of the objectives of a multi-access operating system is to minimize the response time to each user, while a batch system is designed to maximize the amount of processing performed by the system. A user at a terminal requires that his files are secure against hardware and software malfunction and against unauthorized access. The first file management systems were developed to meet these needs.

Interactive computing was carried out by users at teletype terminals, and remote batch job submission was also possible using a remote job entry terminal. A remote job entry terminal typically comprised a volume data input device such as a card reader, a line printer, and an off-line storage device such as a magnetic tape drive.

The developments of job control languages meant that the user could specify his requirements to the system more precisely. The user could instruct the computer as to the sequence in which various tasks were to be performed, and the actions to be taken in the event of an error occurring. The operator's role had changed; he was now beginning to respond to the computer rather than control the sequence in which events took place. In batch systems jobs would be loaded in batches into a job queue before being run. In multi-access systems, jobs would be entered via terminals. The operating system would then be responsible for selecting the order in which jobs would be run.

Modern operating systems
To the user the most noticeable change in modern operating systems is the manner in which he expresses his requirements. Function-based command languages have superseded the more cumbersome job control languages of the earlier operating systems, and graphical systems are now superseding command-based systems.

Multi-access systems have become increasingly popular. The reduced cost of terminals and processors coupled with the increased speed and power of the processors has encouraged a growing trend towards distributed computing. The multi-access systems of today often allow batch jobs to be run as background tasks while the interactive jobs are run as foreground tasks. Similarly many batch systems also provide interactive facilities.

With the growing use of multi-access systems and the increase in the number of jobs entered via terminals, the increased use of direct data entry terminals for the input of volume data, and the increased capacity of disk stores, the operator is left with very little to do. We are moving gradually towards a computer room in which the operator is only required to operate peripherals, for example, supplying the printer with paper or changing magnetic tapes.

There is a growing trend towards connecting computer systems together. There has been an increase in the number of tightly coupled multi-processor systems such as distributed array processors. There is also a tendency towards distributing more processing capability into the peripheral and storage units, thus creating multiprocessors of the master–slave type. More importantly there is an increased trend towards the use of computer networks or loosely coupled systems.

Resource management algorithms are improving all the time. However, one constraint imposed upon the design of these algorithms is that they should consume the minimum storage space and processor time. One objective of an operating system is to make the most efficient possible use of the computer's resources. It should not, therefore, consume too many of these resources itself. More sophisticated algorithms are sometimes available, but are not implemented because they consume more resources than they save. Algorithms which once might have been considered to consume too many resources can now be implemented as a result of the reduction in cost of hardware, the increased power and speed of processors and the increased use of parallelism. The fall in cost of hardware means that many functions once performed by software are now performed directly by hardware.

The microcomputer has had a significant impact upon computing over the last decade. Like the first minicomputers and the first mainframe computers before that, the first microcomputers were all monoprogramming systems. The early attempts to produce multi-user microcomputer systems based upon 8-bit microprocessors did not prove very popular. Multi-user systems based upon the later 16-bit and 32-bit microprocessors are proving much more popular.

The emphasis of all software development nowadays is on ease of use. This is very noticeable in the development of operating systems for microcomputers. The earliest microcomputer operating systems were all command driven, paralleling the trends in mainframe operating systems at the time. The problem with a command-based control language is that the commands have to be learnt by the user before he can make proper use of the system. In order to make the task easier for the user, many systems respond to a command by displaying a menu of options or prompts for each of the parameters. In this way the user need only learn the keywords

and not the formats of the commands. The latest microcomputer systems make use of graphical images representing functions which the user can select with pointers.

An operating system is now an integral part of a computer system. It is an interface between the user's program and the hardware. The operating system is not a single routine but a collection of routines. While the computer system is operating, some of the routines will be resident in main store, others will be held on backing store until required. The routines which are resident in store form the kernel of the operating system.

The facilities provided by an operating system can be summarized as follows.

Resource management

One function of an operating system is to make the most efficent use of the computer system's resources. The objective may be to maximize the amount of processing performed by the computer system or to minimize the response time to individual users. The resources which the operating system is responsible for include

Processor time
Main storage space
File storage space
Peripherals and channels.

Protection

The user can no longer be responsible for the security of his programs and data. In a modern computer system, programs and data are usually held on public disk files which may also be accessed by other users. An operating system must provide protection for a user's program and data files against corruption by software or hardware malfunction and against unauthorized access. It is also important that one program should not corrupt the areas of main store occupied by another program resident at the same time.

User interface

The user's view of the operating system is provided through the job control or command language. This enables the user to specify his requirements to the system. It is important that the language should be easy to understand and use.

4 Hardware interface

The operating system provides an easy interface with the hardware for the user to work with. This is particularly noticeable with input/output transfers. On early computer systems, read and write instructions required the user to perform all the necessary buffering, data conversion and error checking. Now these tasks are all performed by the operating system.

The view of the hardware presented to the user by the operating system is not necessarily the same as the physical configuration of the computer system. Spooling can be used to provide the impression that there are more peripherals than physically exist. Even processor functions can be provided by the operating system. For example, floating-point division might be provided as an operating system routine rather than a hardware unit. Conversely, operating system functions, such as main store memory protection, can be provided by hardware.

5 Accounting information

The operating system can record the usage made of the system by each user. This can vary from recording the amount of processor time used to keeping a detailed record of every resource used – for example, the number of lines of output produced, and the amount of store utilized both on disk and in main memory.

6 Fault diagnosis and error logging

The operating system can assist both the programmer and the engineer by providing diagnostic information about software and hardware faults. A journal is kept of those messages that appear on the operator's console, those output by the operating system or a user's program, and those typed in by the operator. The engineer's log records the machine's status when any error occurs (i.e. register contents, instruction being obeyed).

2 Job control

The purpose of a job control language (JCL) is to enable the user to inform the operating system of his requirements. The user's view of the operating system is provided through the job control language.

On the very earliest computer systems, job control was achieved by inserting control cards between sections of code and data. These cards acted as delimiters to separate code from data as well as instructions to the operating system. As operating systems became more sophisticated and the job control languages of necessity also became more complex, the control cards were separated from the programs and data, and input as a separate job description. The job description is a high-level sequence of instructions informing the operating system of the order in which to run the programs comprising the job. It was considered to be a specialist's task to write these job descriptions. The systems programmers responsible for writing the job descriptions were usually highly revered by their colleagues, to whom JCL was a complete mystery. The format of job control language instructions is often not conducive to general use, as they require specialist knowledge of the computer system not otherwise needed by the user.

With the advent of terminal-based distributed systems and microcomputers, the nature of control languages has changed. The role of the control language is still to inform the operating system of the tasks to be performed, but the instructions are function based rather than job based. A user at a terminal does not have to set up a complete description of a job but can inform the system of each task to be performed.

Control cards

The earliest control programs introduced control cards to reduce the level of operator intervention. The control cards were spaced throughout a pack of cards as separators and to identify the routine required to process the cards that followed. Among the earliest systems to use control cards was the FORTRAN Monitor System (FMS) introduced on the IBM 709 in 1958. Each of the control cards was identified by a dollar in the first column. A typical job might look like the one opposite.

```
$JOB user name, account number, time limit
$FTN
        FORTRAN source
$FAP
        assembler subroutine to be incorporated
        into FORTRAN program
$DATA
        data cards
$EOF
```

Job descriptions

On batch operating systems, jobs are controlled by the instructions contained within a job description. Most of these systems were originally card based and the job descriptions would be submitted on cards. Job descriptions are often submitted in batches. The system can then decide the most effective order in which to run the jobs.

A typical job description will be framed by JOB and ENDJOB records to identify the beginning and the end of the job. The JOB identifier will usually carry further information identifying the user and the account to which the run is to be charged.

A typical job might be set up as

```
JOB user identifier, account number, comment
    job description
ENDJOB
```

The user identifier and account number are assigned by the system manager.

The job will consist of a number of processes to be performed, where each process is likely to be a a user program or a utility. Job control instructions are required for each program and will inform the operating system of

1 The resources required to run the program
2 Where the program is held
3 Events that might occur during the running of a program and the corresponding actions to be obeyed (event list).

The job will consist of one or more programs which are usually to be run in sequence. Some operating systems permit multiprogramming between jobs but not between the programs within a job, while other operating systems assume that programs within a job will be multiprogrammed unless specifically prevented (such as when an output file from one program is to be used as the input file to a second program). In such cases the programs must be run in sequence.

Specifying resources
The user is able to specify the following

The storage requirements   When a program is compiled and all the necessary subroutines have been linked, the size of the object program will be known. This will be the amount of storage space allocated to the program unless a STORE command is specified in the job description. For example, STORE 32678 specifies that 32 678 words/bytes of store are to be allocated for this run. This command can only be of any advantage when variable-sized arrays or lists have been declared in the program or when overlaying of segments is used.
An execution time limit   This is used to specify how many seconds of processor time the program is likely to use. For example, TIME 5 indicates that execution is to be terminated after 5 seconds of CPU time. This is a very useful feature for ensuring that programs under test do not waste processor time executing uncontrolled loops.
Peripheral and file requirements   Some operat-

ing systems require that all peripheral and file requirements are specified in the job description, whereas others require only slow peripherals to be specified in advance. In a system which uses spooled input it is important to specify slow peripherals in advance, in order to determine that the input file has been spooled in prior to running the program. In some systems it is necessary to specify which files are required in order that the operating system can check that the tapes and disks containing the files are mounted. Some early systems even required the user to specify the exact location of the files (e.g. the volume number, cylinder number and track number of the first block of the file). Specifying file requirements is not a prerequisite of all systems.

Specifying the program or process
To some systems user programs, compilers and utilities are all programs. Other systems differentiate between a user program and systems software; they use the term 'program' for user programs only, and the term 'process' to cover both user programs and systems software.

In most systems, specifying a process such as compilation is achieved by means of a COMPILE command, for example,

COMPILE program name, language code

or by a command such as

FORTCOMPILE program name

In these examples, compilation is treated as a special process. However, in some systems all programs are treated alike and a compiler must be loaded in the same way as any other program. For example, on the ICL 2903 series, specifying a COBOL compilation would require

IN ED(PROGRAM XEC2)   the disk file containing the compiler
LOAD #XEC2   the subfile to be loaded
ENTER 1   the entry point of the compiler.

Specifying an event list

All programs need to communicate with the operating system even if it is only to inform the system that the run has finished. Many programs need to communicate with the operator, for example to request the generation number of a file. The actions to be taken when these external events occur can be written into the job description. The job control instructions can be used to differentiate between normal and abnormal termination. In the event of normal termination of a program, the next program can be loaded; or in the case of abnormal termination, the job control can be used to print out diagnostic information. The answers to many of the requests issued by a program can be written into the job description.

Job control languages

Job control languages differ from programming languages in several respects:

1 The format of the commands in many of the early job control languages were primitive, and did not permit the control instructions to be structured in the way that a program might be. Sequences of control statements could be written but most job control languages had only limited facilities for conditional instructions and often no facilities at all for incorporating iterations. Later job control languages became more sophisticated and permitted job descriptions to be structured in the same manner as programs.

2 A detailed knowledge of the computer system was often required to be able to write the job description that was not necessarily required by the user when writing a program.

3 Job control languages have not achieved the same degree of portability as programming languages.

Job description macros

On most systems it is possible to store complete or partially complete job descriptions in a directory. Each of these job descriptions is assigned a unique name. A stored job description can then be included in a job by referring to the unique name. The stored job descriptions are usually known as macros. Parameters may be passed to these macros in much the same way as parameters may be passed to a subroutine.

Command languages

With the advent of terminal-based computer systems and microcomputers, the nature of command languages has changed. The user may still build up a job as a sequence of commands, but it is more likely that he will build up a job as he sits at the keyboard, typing in commands which immediately invoke action from the system.

The user must establish contact with the system at the beginning of a session. This is achieved by typing in a unique user name and a secret password to identify the user to the system. This process is called *logging on*. The system will respond with a prompt character inviting the user to type in a command. The action invoked by this command will then be performed by the system.

All command-based control languages have a similar repertoire of commands, based upon the functions that a user is likely to require.

The repertoire of commands will include facilities for

> File manipulation
> File management
> Obtaining information about the system.

The format of each command is usually a mnemonic, which is used to identify the function required, followed by a string of parameters (where appropriate); for example,

> EDIT myprog

The user at a terminal is in greater control of the execution of his program than the user of a batch system. This is particularly important during the development stages of a program. The user can often detect that things are going wrong during the early stages of a test run, and the run can be aborted. For example, trivial syntax errors which prevent a program from compiling can be easily corrected, permitting the program to be recompiled before testing.

File manipulation commands
The most frequently invoked commands will be those which manipulate files. A file may contain the source or object version of a program, the data that is to be used or produced by the program, or even the compiler to be used to translate the program into object code. Within this catagory are those commands which invoke routines to operate upon the files. The most commonly used file manipulation commands perform the following tasks:

Editing a file   All computer systems require a facility for creating and altering files, and this is usually performed by a text editor. Most on-line systems provide the user with facilities for editing text files, as described in Chapter 4. To invoke the editor, the user simply types a mnemonic, such as EDIT, followed by the name of the file; for example,

> EDIT myprog

where myprog is the name of the file.

Compiling a program   The process of translating a program from its source version into its

object version can normally be invoked by typing a single command. The command will usually indicate the language in which the program is written; for example,

> COBOL myprog

Linking subroutines to the object program   The object code produced by a compiler is not, generally speaking, in a suitable state for execution. It will, almost certainly, contain references to library subroutines and to subroutines written by the user. The object versions of the subroutines must be linked to the object code of the program before the program can be executed. The task is performed by a linkage editor (also known as a task builder or consolidator). This routine will be invoked by a command such as

> LINK myprog

The linkage editor will automatically scan the system library for standard subroutines, but if user-defined subroutines are also to be incorporated then the libraries containing these routines must be specified.

Running the program   To execute a program the user types a command such as RUN; for example,

> RUN myprog

Listing a file   One of the more commonly required functions is to list text files; for example,

> LIST myprog

The user is often provided with the option of listing the file at the terminal or directing the output to a remote printer.

The file type need not usually be specified. It is only necessary to specify the type if it differs from the default value assumed for the command. (The syntax of the commands varies from system to system.)

File management commands
When a user 'logs on' to the system he will be put in contact with his own user directory (see Chapter 4). Most of the file management com-

mands relate to this user file directory. The commands that the user will require relate to the following:

The creation and deletion of directories On a system with a hierarchical file directory structure (see Chapter 4) a user may create subdirectories to his own directory. It is important to remember that when a directory is deleted all of its subdirectories and files will also be deleted.

Creating and deleting files Facilities are often provided for creating a new file using the text editor or by a special 'create file' command. Deleting a file is not usually provided as a function of the editor but by a separate 'delete file' command. This reduces the probability of a file being deleted by mistake.

Changing the password to a directory This should be done at regular intervals as a matter of course.

Copying and renaming files It is often advantageous to edit a copy of a file and thus preserve the source version of a working program.

Commands used to provide information

The user is usually provided with a number of commands which he can use to obtain information such as the current date and the time, the amount of CPU time that a process has used, and details about the amount of disk space used by his files.

The system will provide a command to print a catalogue of the files contained within a user's directory. The amount of information printed out about each directory entry will vary from system to system, but all systems provide a cataloguing facility. The catalogue function will print out the name and type of each file listed in the directory. It may also print out details such as the file size,

the date the file was last altered and the access rights for various categories of user.

Practically all systems provide one command which is of particular benefit to users new to the system. This is the HELP command. The HELP command will provide the user with further information on how to use all the other commands. The HELP utility leads the user through a series of questions in order to provide him with the information he requires.

Command procedures

Sequences of commands may be strung together to create command procedures. The command procedure will be held in a file and assigned a name. Any of the commands available to the user sitting at a terminal may be used in a command procedure. A typical command procedure might be to compile, link and test a COBOL program. Firstly a file must be created which contains the commands. Consider the following example of a VAX/VMS command procedure:

```
$COBOL   myprog
$LINK    myprog
$RUN     myprog
```

where myprog is the name of the file containing the program. If we suppose that the command sequence is held in a file called MYTEST which must be of type COM (for COMMAND), then when we wish to invoke the command procedure we must inform the system that the file contains a command sequence. This is done by means of a special character preceding the filename, e.g. @MYTEST.

By using a system variable in place of the filename myprog in the example above, the command procedure can be made more general. As well as allowing the use of variables within a command procedure, many systems allow the inclusion of conditional and iterative statements.

Current developments

The latest generation of microcomputer operating systems have adopted a different approach towards interfacing with the user.

Graphical images called *icons*, which represent the facilities available, are displayed upon the screen. Selecting the function to be performed is achieved by selecting the appropriate icon.

On machines such as Apple's Lisa the first display that greets the user is the desktop, so called because the icons displayed represent items usually found on or around the top of a desk, such as file folders, a clipboard and a wastebasket. To select an icon, a pointer is moved so that its arrowhead touches any part of the icon. On the Lisa, movement of the pointer is achieved by a device called a mouse, which can be used on any flat surface. A wire connects the mouse to the computer and a ball bearing enables it to move around. When the mouse is moved, the pointer moves in the corresponding direction on the screen. A button on the top of the mouse is used to select an icon.

To access a file, the file system icon must be selected. On the Lisa the file system icon is called the profile. To open the profile the user selects the file/print title which appears in the top left-hand corner of the screen. This causes the file/print menu to be displayed. A menu is a list of operations that may be performed; among these operations will be the option to open the icon selected, in this case the profile. When a menu item has been selected it will be highlighted, i.e. displayed as white characters on a black back-

ground rather than the more usual dark characters on a light background.

When the profile has been opened, the profile window will appear on the screen. A window is used to view the contents of an icon. Each file within the profile is also represented by an icon seen through the window. The files may contain data, user-written programs or packages. If the profile contains more files than can be viewed through the window then the image displayed can be scrolled.

The contents of the window can be moved up, down, left or right. The size of the window can be altered and several different windows can be displayed simultaneously. Windows can be allowed to overlap or occupy separate portions of the screen. Only the latest window accessed will be active. It is only within this window that icons may be selected or the image scrolled. An icon selected from the profile window could represent a data file which is to be edited, or a user program to be compiled, or one of the standard packages which is to be run, such as the word processing, database or graphics package. When the icon has been selected, the menu is used to determine the operation to be performed.

Job scheduling

The different operating environments of a batch operating system and a multi-access operating system dictate different scheduling requirements. In a traditional batch environment the user will write a job description to indicate his requirements. In a multi-access environment the user will dictate his requirements from the terminal. A job scheduler in a batch system can organize the jobs to maximize the throughput of the machine, which may mean allocating resources to one job at the expense of another. In this way the execution of one job may be delayed for a considerable time. A multi-access system will often be processing both batch and interactive tasks. Terminal users will frequently be performing highly interactive tasks such as editing files while batch jobs such as

spooling input and output are run simultaneously as background tasks. The user may wish to initiate batch jobs from the terminal. The user expects a near immediate response to interactive tasks; the scheduler must, therefore, attempt to satisfy all users and provide each with the impression that he is the only user. This can often be achieved at the expense of the overall amount of processing carried out by the machine. The type of scheduler, therefore, will be dictated by the environment.

The task of the scheduler is to select which of a number of programs currently 'being executed' is to have control of the central processor.

The programs waiting to be executed may already be in main store or may be on backing store. In a batch system, only the programs in main store will be considered for selection. This avoids incurring the high time penalties caused by frequently transferring programs or segments of programs between backing store and main store. When a program terminates or releases storage space or peripherals, then one or more of the programs waiting on backing store may be transferred into the main memory. The process of selecting which program is to be executed is performed by a low-level scheduler; the process of selecting which program(s) to transfer from backing store into main store is performed by a high-level scheduler. In a multi-access system the requirements are different; the scheduler cannot be restricted to selecting one of the programs already in main store. The number of programs waiting to be executed is dictated by the number of users currently on-line. It is quite probable that the amount of storage space occupied by all these programs will exceed the amount of storage space available. The constraints upon a scheduler in a multi-access environment are different: the scheduler must attempt to maximize the throughput of the machine but with the single overriding proviso that each user must receive attention at frequent intervals.

In a paged memory system (see Chapter 3) the characteristics of a batch or multi-access environment are not altered but the number of programs that may be supported in main store is increased. A better use of resources is provided in both cases. In a batch environment it is now necessary to transfer pages between main store and backing store, but the level of multiprogramming (the number of programs being considered for selection by the scheduler) is increased. In a multi-access environment the level of multiprogramming is fixed by the number of users, but the unit of transfer between main store and backing store is reduced from whole programs or segments of programs to a page.

Low-level scheduler

In a batch system each program is allocated a priority. This priority can be based upon estimations of resource usage, such as time limits, memory utilization, number of files and the volume of input/output. The priority assigned to a program may, however, be based upon factors beyond the realm of the operating systems, such as the 'importance' of the program or the influence of the user. The scheduler maintains a list of the programs in the machine's memory and the status of each program, indicating whether

The program is suspended and the reason for the suspension, e.g. awaiting completion of a peripheral transfer
The program is free to run
The program is actually running.

The scheduler will examine this list every time an interrupt occurs. The program selected will be the one that has the highest priority of those free to run. This may be the program that was running when the interrupt occurred.

The effect of priority allocation can best be illustrated through an extreme example. Consider two programs represented by C and S. Program C is a commercial program involving a lot of input and output. Program S is a scentific program which has no input or output. The priority is based upon the volume of input and output.

If program S is given the higher priority then program S will run to completion before program C begins (Figure 7).

If, however, program C is given the higher priority then each time that program C is suspended program S will be processed. The peripheral-dependent program will be suspended at frequent intervals, allowing the 'number crunching' program to be executed (Figure 8). As can be seen from the figures, greater utilization of the processor can be achieved by giving higher priorities to a program involving a much larger amount of input and output. The processor-dependent program should be allocated a low

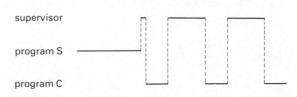

Figure 7   *Program S priority*

priority and the peripheral-dependent program should be allocated a high priority.

Consider the example in Figure 9 of three programs running simultaneously. We can assume that program X has the highest priority and that program Z has the lowest priority. During the time interval shown on the figure, seven interrupts i_1–i_7 occur:

i_1 Program X issues a read instruction and cannot continue until the data has been input. Program X is, therefore, suspended and program Y is run.

i_2 Program Y issues a read instruction, program Y is in turn suspended and program Z commences.

i_3 The read instruction issued by program X has terminated. Program X is once again free to run and may resume control.

i_4 The read instruction issued by program Y is completed, but although program Y is now free to run it is not the program with the highest priority and program X continues.

i_5 Program X issues a second read instruction involving a peripheral transfer (see 'Blocking' in Chapter 3) and program Y takes over.

i_6 An interrupt occurs which does not affect the status of the program running, e.g. an operator changing a disk.

i_7 The second read instruction issued by program X is completed and the program is free to continue.

The allocation of priorities to a program is not an easy task, particularly as the priority values allocated are not absolute but are relative values to be compared with other programs in store. It is easy to determine that a print program should have a higher priority than a program to calculate π to 1000 decimal places, but the relative priorities

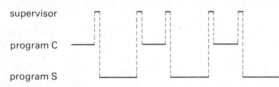

Figure 8   *Program C priority*

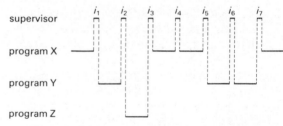

Figure 9   *Three programs: X highest, Z lowest priority*

of two peripheral-dependent programs is harder to determine. A program which performs all its input first and then processes this data before printing out the results really requires three different priorities to reflect the changing stages of the program. Because it is so difficult to obtain the correct mix of program priorities, many installations pay scant regard to allocating priorities; for example, all COBOL programs may be awarded the same priority.

High-level scheduler

The purpose of the high-level scheduler is to select which of the programs in the job queue should be loaded into the main store. There may be several programs held in the job queue waiting to be run, but a program can only be loaded if it satisfies all of the following criteria:

1   There is sufficient storage space available in which to load the program.
2   All the input files required by the program have already been spooled in.
3   All other peripherals required by the program are available.
4   Any other programs which must be completed first have already been run.

The next program to be loaded will be selected from the programs which satisfy the above criteria on the basis of:

1   The program nearest to the front of the job queue (this is the simplest philosophy to implement).
2   The program which makes the least demand upon the systems resources. This selection is made on the basis that another program may then be loaded using the remaining resources, so large programs with heavy peripheral

requirements may wait for some time before being loaded.

3 The program which can make the maximum utilization of the available resources. This method of selection gives a favourable opportunity for large programs to be loaded and is balanced by the availability of resources.

A priority-based system. Each program is allocated a loading priority. Higher priority programs are considered first, and the priority of each program is uprated every time it is passed over.

Scheduling in a multi-access system

In a multi-access system, each user connected to the system must appear to receive the same response. The simplest way in which to achieve this is to maintain a list of all programs being run and to work through the list allocating each process an equal slice of processor time. This system, often known as a 'round-robin' system, is much favoured in multi-access systems. There is, however, a problem in that the total storage requirements of all the users will exceed the main store capacity and lead to programs being stored on backing storage between turns at being processed. Each time a program is processed it involves two tranfers between backing store and main store – one to move the program in store out to make space for the incoming program, and the second to bring the program into store. Working out the size of the time slice is, therefore, a carefully calculated balance between minimizing the number of data transfers which can be achieved by increasing the time slice and providing a reasonable response time for the user, i.e. ensuring that each user's program is processed within a given response time.

If the time spent transferring programs to and from store can be reduced then more time becomes available for processing programs.

The two techniques described below are designed to improve system performance by reducing the time spent swapping programs in and out of store.

Multilevel scheduling algorithm
This technique is based upon granting interactive

jobs frequent short bursts of CPU time, whereas batch tasks are granted longer but less frequent time slices. This is achieved by keeping more than one list of programs. The separate lists are considered as having different priorities. Programs from the lower-priority lists are only run when the higher-priority lists are empty.

Programs may be initially allocated to any of the lists; they are usually allocated to a list according to the nature of the task. Each list may have its own scheduling algorithm. Programs in list 1 may be selected on a 'first come, first served' basis. Programs which enter list 1 may pre-empt programs from lower lists which are already running. A program from list 1 may be given a very short slice of CPU time. When this allocated time slice has been used up the program will be placed on the bottom of list 2. The scheduler will then select the next program from the top of list 1. If list 1 is empty then the program at the top of list 2 will be selected. Programs in list 2 may be scheduled on a 'round-robin' basis. When list 2 is also empty, a program from list 3 will be selected. Programs from list 3 might be scheduled on a priority basis.

When a program selected from list 2 or 3 completes its time slice it may be placed back on the bottom of the same list. The number of times that a program may be placed back on the same list is determined by the system manager. The number of times is the same for all programs in the list, and when a program has used all of the allocated number of time slices in one list it will be moved down a level to the next list. The number of lists and the time slice for each list are also determined by the system manager (Figure 10).

This system favours shorter interactive jobs but allows longer-running batch jobs to share the resources. The system reduces the amount of time spent transferring longer-running programs to

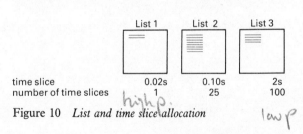

	List 1	List 2	List 3
time slice	0.02s	0.10s	2s
number of time slices	1	25	100

Figure 10 *List and time slice allocation*

and from main store by granting the programs from list 3 longer time slices when they are eventually selected. This system was originally developed for the Compatible Time-Sharing System (CTSS) and was also used on the DEC PDP10 system.

The UNIX scheduler
The UNIX operating system uses a time slice algorithm that is based not on a round-robin approach but upon a system of priorities. The priority of a program is determined by a calculation based upon the amount of execution time each program has used since it was last brought into store. A program that has only just been brought into store has had little opportunity to use processor time and consequently has a high priority.

A program which has received a lot of execution time will have been rolled out on to backing store and will not be brought back into store until other programs have received a similar amount of time. When a program is brought into store, its accumulated time is reset to zero. UNIX takes into account the fact that a program waiting for an input/output transfer to be completed will not be able to take advantage of its turn.

Scheduling multiprocessor systems
The scheduling algorithms described above relate to a single processor; however, many computer systems today contain multiple processors. These processors will not necessarily be the same. If the processors are of different types then it is quite likely that jobs will have to be scheduled for a particular processor. In this case each processor will have its own job queue and its own scheduler. If there are several identical processors then maintaining separate job queues and separately scheduling each processor makes inefficient use of the resources. It is far better to schedule the processors from a single job queue.

There are two approaches to scheduling jobs when there are several identical processors. One approach is to designate one of the processors as the scheduler and to treat the other processors as resources to be allocated. Alternatively each processor may select its own jobs from the job queue. If the second approach is adopted, care must be taken to ensure that a job is not selected by more than one processor and that jobs do not get left in the job queue.

Exercises

2.1 Compare the use of command languages with job control languages.

2.2 In a batch system, which has four programs running, a priority-based low-level scheduler is selecting the order in which the programs are being run. Draw a timing diagram, using the following format, to show the sequence in which the programs are executed (the program priorities are shown in brackets). You may assume that the program being executed is always suspended when it issues a read or write instruction.

Supervisor	i_1	i_2	i_3	i_4	i_5	i_6	i_7	i_8	i_9	i_{10}
Program A (80)										
Program B (70)										
Program C (60)										
Program D (50)										

The following is the sequence of events:

i_1 The program running issues a read instruction which involves a peripheral transfer from a magnetic tape file.

i_2 The program running issues a write instruction to a magnetic disk file.

i_3 The write instruction to a disk file is completed.

i_4 The attempt to read from the tape file has failed due to a parity error; the program is terminated.

i_5 The program running issues a write instruction to a magnetic disk file.

i_6 The write instruction to the disk file is completed.

i_7 The operator changes the priority of program D to 75.

i_8 The program running issues a read instruction to a spooled input file.

i_9 The program running fails due to a divide error.

i_{10} The read instruction to a spooled input file is completed.

2.3 A multi-access system is using a multilevel scheduler. The current state of the programs' lists is:

	List 1	List 2	List 3
	—	Program D (2)	Program B (1)
		Program C (3)	Program A (2)
Time slice	0.02 s	0.20 s	2.00 s
Number of time slices	1	5	Unlimited

The number of time slices each program has received in its current list is shown in brackets. The order in which the programs have been executed so far is:

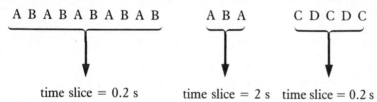

A B A B A B A B A B   A B A   C D C D C

time slice = 0.2 s   time slice = 2 s   time slice = 0.2 s

Show the sequence in which the programs will be executed for the next 9 seconds and the state of the lists at the end of the 9 second period.

good

block = 64 or 128 words of store

1 byte = 8 bits 16

24 bits = 1 word

3 bytes = 1 word

3 Memory and device management systems

Memory management systems

One of the most important functions of a multiprogramming control program is the management of the main storage areas. The major objectives of a memory management system are

1 Ensuring that memory space is used efficiently.
2 Address mapping; this is the translation of program addresses into storage locations.
3 Protecting the area of store occupied by a program against corruption by other users.
4 Allocating storage space to programs.

Utilization of memory space

Storage space is allocated to programs in blocks of store. A block of store corresponds to the area of store locked out during a peripheral transfer and is typically 64 or 128 words of store. In a conventional memory the program will be allocated sufficient contiguous blocks of store to accommodate the program. The memory allocation routine will search the main memory for an area of store large enough to accommodate the program. The basis on which the area is selected will be considered later, but the area of store chosen is likely to be larger than is required. When the program has been allocated the storage space it requires, the area of store left over may be too small to use.

Most programs that are written contain loops of instructions which are obeyed repeatedly. To execute this loop of instructions may take several intervals of processor time. During this period the rest of the program is occupying space that could be advantageously used by other programs. If the storage requirements of each program can be reduced to hold just the instructions and data currently being referenced, then the number of programs sharing the memory space can be increased.

There are two different approaches to partitioning a program in order to reduce its storage requirements. These are the logical approach, whereby the program is separated into logically distinct sections of code called segments, and the physical approach, in which the system divides the program into identically sized sections called pages. The programmer may organize his code into segments of varying size reflecting the logic of the problem being solved. The compiler may generate more than one segment from the source code input by creating separate segments for global variables, for each procedure or function and for the main body of the program. The segments are usually compiled separately, which means that in high-level languages segments can only be written as subroutines. If two or more segments are mutually exclusive then it is not necessary to reserve storage space for both segments. Providing an area is reserved which is large enough to accommodate the biggest segment, only one area need be reserved. This area is known as an overlay area because, when a new segment is called in, it replaces the segment already there. It is thought of as being placed on top of the existing code; hence the term 'overlay'.

Paging, unlike segmentation, should be invisible to the programmer. The instruction and data areas of the program are divided into fixed-size blocks called pages. The main memory is also divided into areas of the same size, called page frames. Only a few pages of each program will be in store at a time.

Address mapping

In a multiprogramming environment several programs will be sharing the memory space. The mix of programs will be continuously changing and a user cannot predict which other programs will be running with his. Whereabouts in memory a program is loaded will depend upon the memory space available at the time. Addresses within a program cannot refer to absolute memory locations as the program may be loaded anywhere in store. The program addresses must be expressed relative to the start of the program area and converted into absolute store addresses at run time.

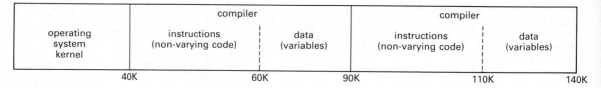

operating system kernel	compiler		compiler	
	instructions (non-varying code)	data (variables)	instructions (non-varying code)	data (variables)

40K   60K   90K   110K   140K

Figure 11   *Compiler copies: storage map*

Addressing within a conventional memory

Base/limit register systems

One of the most widely favoured techniques makes use of base and limit registers. The *base register* is used in the conversion of program addresses. All program addresses are compiled as displacements from the beginning of the program. When the program is loaded into memory the absolute address of the start of the program (the first memory location it occupies) is stored as the value for the base register. Program addresses are then converted into addresses by adding the contents of the base register to the compiled addresses. The *limit register* is used to ensure that all memory accesses refer to locations within the memory space allocated to the program.

Many computer systems have only one physical pair of base and limit registers. The base and limit register values for a program will be transferred into the actual registers when the program is to be executed. Base/limit registers allow the memory management system to place a program anywhere in store.

Some systems provide two base/limit register pairs, which allows the memory management system to make even more efficient use of the memory. One base/limit register pair will normally be used for the program instructions and the other for the data; then the program and data do not have to occupy one contiguous area of store but can be allocated two separate areas.

In a multiprogramming system, there is a high probability that more than one user will be using the same systems program, such as a compiler. If there are two copies of a compiler present in store at the same time then there is a considerable duplication of code. If the compiler is separated into one part which contains pure procedures and constant items of data and a second part which contains variable items of data, then the two copies of the compiler can be shown as in Figure 11. (A pure procedure is a section of code that does not alter during its execution.)

As far as the system is concerned, two versions of the compiler are running. The base/limit register values are:

	Instruction		*Data*	
	Base	Limit	Base	Limit
User 1	40K	20K	60K	30K
User 2	90K	20K	110K	30K

There is no need to hold two copies of the compiler code in store. The instruction parts of the two compilers are identical. By making use of the two base/limit register pairs, only one copy of the compiler code need be held in store. The instruction base register for both users can refer to the same area of store.

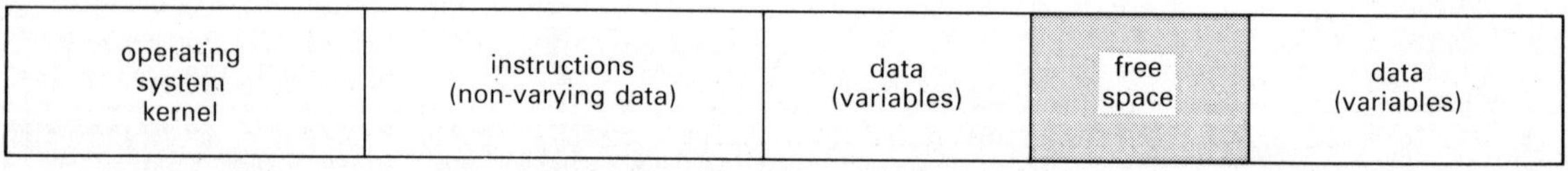

operating system kernel	instructions (non-varying data)	data (variables)	free space	data (variables)

Figure 12   *New storage map, using two base/limit register pairs*

	Instruction		Data	
	Base	Limit	Base	Limit
User 1	40K	20K	60K	30K
User 2	40K	20K	110K	30K

The storage requirements are now reduced; this can be shown by considering the new storage map (Figure 12).

If users are sharing segments of code then the memory management system must not release an area of store until the last user's program has terminated.

Base and displacement addressing
The IBM 370 does not use a special base register but one of the sixteen general purpose registers under programmer control. The programmer specifies which register is to be used and must include instructions to assign a value to the register. For example,

BALR 12,0   Load register 12 with address of next instruction.

USING *, 12   Inform the assembler which register is being used as the base register.

All operand addresses are compiled as a displacement from the base register.

All operands addressed by this base register must be declared within the 4095 bytes that follow the specification of the base register. To access operands beyond this limit, the user must specify another base register.

Addressing within a segmented memory system
If a program has been written as a number of separately compiled segments, then the addresses within each segment must be translated into memory locations. Each program address is given as two parts – a segment number and the address within the segment. These addresses can be mapped into storage locations by using a segment table (Figure 13).

Each entry in the segment table is known as a segment descriptor. The segment descriptor will contain the base address and size of each segment and protection bits which indicate the type of access that may be made to the segment. If a segment has not yet been loaded into store, then the segment table will contain the address of the segment on backing store. A memory bit indicates whether the segment is held in main store or on backing store. If one segment attempts to transfer control to another segment or access an element within another segment, then the segment part of the address will be used as an index to the

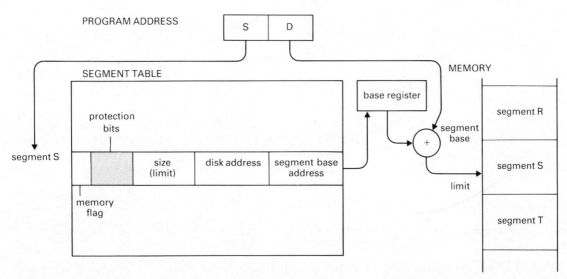

Figure 13   *Addressing in a segmented memory system. S: segment number. D: address within segment*

segment table. The segment descriptor accessed will indicate whether or not the segment is in store. If the segment is not in main memory, the program will be suspended while the segment is loaded. The segment will not be loaded if the program is attempting to access the segment in a way that is not permitted by the protection bits. The protection bits indicate whether read, write or execute access is allowed. If the access being made is permitted and the segment has been loaded, then the base and limit values will be loaded into the base/limit registers. Access to another segment can only be made via a special entry point.

Addressing within a paged memory

In a paged memory system the program is divided into fixed-size blocks called pages. The store is divided into blocks of the same size called page frames. Each program will have only a few pages in store at a time. These pages need not represent a continuous section of code and they need not occupy contiguous page frames. The addresses within the program must be converted into memory addresses. If the program addresses have been compiled as a displacement from the

beginning of the program, then each address has two parts:

page number	displacement within page
0 5	6 15

If 16 bits are used to represent each address then the first six bits represent the logical page number and the remaining ten bits can identify a location within the page (assuming a page size of 1024 locations).

Using a page size, which can be expressed as 2^n words/bytes (where n is integer), means that the least significant n bits of the address will give the displacement within the page.

To convert a program address into a memory address, the page number must be converted into the page frame number of the frame containing the page. This can be performed using a page table, which will hold the page frame numbers of any pages held in main store and the addresses of all pages on backing store (Figure 14).

The location required can be accessed faster using an associative memory to identify the page frame number. The associative memory, alterna-

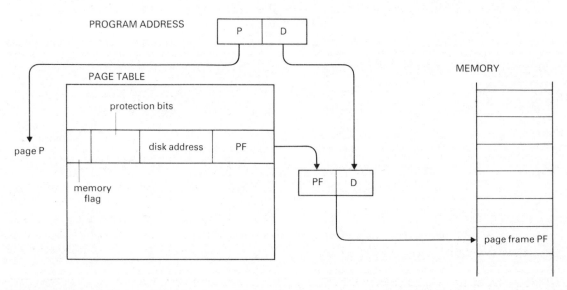

Figure 14   *Paged memory addressing using page table. P: page number. PF: page frame number. D: displacement within page*

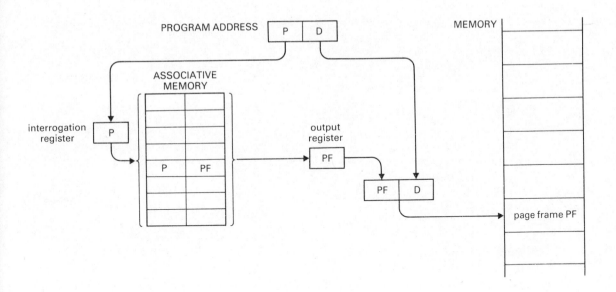

Figure 15   *Paged addressing using associative memory*

tively known as a contents addressable memory, is a small, very fast memory which contains the logical page number and the corresponding page frame numbers for the most recently accessed pages.

An associative memory does not use an address in the conventional manner to access the required location, but uses part of the location's contents as a key to unlock the remainder of the contents. The required page number is used as the key, which is compared simultaneously with all the stored page numbers. If a match is found, then the remainder of the contents, in this case the page frame number, are placed in the associative memory's output register. The associative memory is constructed using the fastest memory technology available, and is consequently small to minimize costs (ICL 2900 series is 64 words, and the larger IBM 370 series is 128 words). See Figure 15.

The associative memory will contain the page frame numbers of the most recently referenced pages. If a page is not located through the associative memory then the page must be accessed using the page tables.

The necessity to access locations using an associative memory or page and segment tables slows down individual memory accesses. On the other hand, the use of segmentation and paging permits a greater number of programs to share the main memory. The time taken to search the associative memory will be small by comparison with the time taken to search the page and segmentation tables.

The techniques of segmentation and paging can be combined to provide the advantages that both techniques offer. Each segment can be compiled separately and have its own page table. When the various segments are bound together by the linkage editor, a segment table is created, which contains the address of the page table created for each segment. Addresses are in three parts – the segment number, the page number and the location within the page. See Figure 16.

The location of the page frame containing the required page may be found from the associative memory. If the page cannot be located through the associative memory then it will be accessed via the segment and page tables.

Accessing a page via the page and segment tables can be very time consuming. The relevant tables may be on backing store and so will have to be

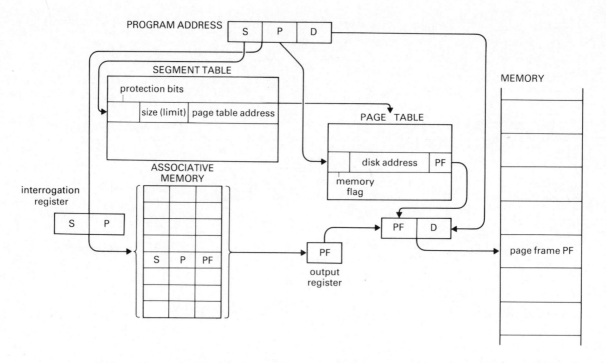

Figure 16 *Combined segmentation and paging*

brought into main store before the page can be located.

Protection

When several programs co-reside in the same memory space, it is essential that one program should not be permitted to corrupt the program space of another. It is equally important that a user's program should not corrupt the memory space of the operating system. The operating system, however, will require access to the memory space allocated to the user's program. It is not possible for all memory accesses to be checked at compile time, as in many cases the addresses will not be known until run time; for example, an array may not be given dimensions until run time. All memory accesses, whether fetching an instruction or an operand, must be checked at run time to ensure that the location is within the memory space allocated to the program.

Protection in a base/limit register system
The limit register is used to ensure that all memory accesses refer to locations within the storage space allocated to the program (e.g. ICL 1900 series). The limit register may contain either the size of the program or the absolute address of the last memory location. Before any memory access is permitted, the address is compared with the contents of the limit register to ensure that the address lies within the program's allocated area.

If the limit register contains the size of the program then all program addresses must be compared with the limit value before the base address value is added to each program address; these two tasks can be performed in parallel.

Protection key systems
In this system (e.g. IBM 370) the main memory is subdivided into fixed-size blocks. Associated with each block is a four-bit protection register. Each process is assigned a four-bit protection key and

every block of store allocated to the process holds the same four-bit key in its protection register. A process may only access a location if the protection key of the process matches that of the block containing the location. Four bits permits sixteen different keys. Protection key 0000 is reserved for the control program; protection key 1111 is used to indicate blocks of free space.

Control program protection

It is important that no user program should be allowed to corrupt the instructions or data areas of the control program. Ultimate protection of the control program code areas can be achieved by holding the code in a read-only-memory (ROM). This technique is restrictive if the control program has to be modified. Read-only-memory can obviously not be used to protect the control program's data areas.

In a system that employs base/limit registers, the base register value is added to the address of every memory location accessed by the program. This prevents the program accessing any storage location that precedes the first location of the program.

A single bit register can be associated with each block or segment of code, which can be set to indicate that the area can only be accessed by the control program.

Ring protection

A ring protection system extends the concept of control program protection to a hierarchical structure of several levels. The ring protection system is used in conjunction with a base/limit register system. Each segment is assigned a level of privilege (Figure 17). A program may access segments at a different level providing the privilege level of the segment being accessed is greater than or equal to that of the segment making the access. The highest level of privilege (zero) is reserved for the kernel of the operating system. Ring protection systems have been used on the MULTICS system (nine levels) and on the ICL 2900 (sixteen levels).

Storage lockout

An area of store involved in a data transfer must

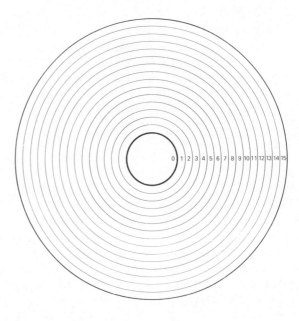

Figure 17   *Ring protection*

be protected to ensure that data being output is not overwritten before the transfer is completed and that an area destined to receive data is not accessed before the data arrives. Storage locations cannot be protected individually, so protection is applied to blocks of store. A single bit register can be used as a flag to indicate that a block of store is 'locked out' for the duration of a peripheral transfer. A more sophisticated system can be achieved by using two flags. One flag will be set if any location within the block is involved in an input data transfer (i.e. the contents of the block are being altered). When this flag is set the block is locked out, thus preventing all other access. The second flag is set if any location within the block is being used by a write statement. As the contents of the block are not altered by an output data transfer, the block need not be completely locked out. The contents of the block can still be accessed by any instruction which does not alter the contents. The IBM 360 used a single flag and the IBM 370 uses two flags.

Allocating storage space in a conventional memory

Placement policies

When storage space is allocated to whole programs or segments the store becomes fragmented. As some programs terminate and new programs are loaded, the unused memory space becomes scattered throughout the memory.

The memory management system must maintain a list of all the areas of unused memory together with their size. When a program terminates, the memory management system must return the storage space released to the free space list. If an area of store released is adjacent to an existing area of free store then the memory management system should recognize that they form a single large area rather than two small areas.

The memory management system must examine the list to see if another program can be loaded, either when a program enters the job queue or when a program terminates. The algorithm that searches the free space list to determine which area of store a program or segment should be loaded into is known as the placement policy. Some of the better-known placement policies are described below.

First-fit policy   The first-fit algorithm maintains the list of free spaces in order of start addresses. The list will be searched from the beginning and a program will be placed in the first free area into which it will fit. If the area is larger than necessary the remaining free space will be returned to the free space list. As the list is kept in memory address order and contains the size of each free area, it is very easy to determine when two adjacent areas are free and combine them into a single entry in the free space list. A variation on the first-fit algorithm is to search the free space list, not from the beginning each time, but cyclically from the point at which the last search finished.

Best-fit policy   The best-fit algorithm maintains the list of free space in order of size, smallest first. By searching the list from the beginning the smallest area into which the program will fit can be found. To avoid the problem of very small areas of free space bunching at the beginning of the list, any free space remaining after a program has been loaded will only be returned to the list if it is large enough to be of any use. Returning areas to the list entails searching the list to find adjacent areas, so that they may be combined into a single larger area.

Worst-fit policy   Working on exactly the opposite principle to the policy above, the worst-fit policy maintains the list of free spaces in order of size, with the largest first. The principle is that a program will be loaded into the largest area of free space. Therefore, the space remaining after this load is more likely to be able to accommodate another program. The problem with this method is that it does not preserve the larger areas of free space and, as a consequence, should a large program require loading, there is unlikely to be a free area which is large enough.

Dynamic relocation

One way to avoid fragmentation is to use a dynamic relocation algorithm:

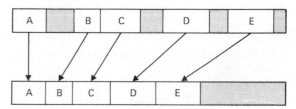

By moving all the segments towards the lower addresses, a single contiguous area of free space is released in the upper region of the store. Although it is only necessary to change the base address and to move the stored instructions and data values down into the lower regions of the store, this is a very time-consuming operation. As a consequence, dynamic relocation is used in conjunction with one of the above policies. Dynamic relocation will only be used to compact the segments when a single fragment large enough cannot be found. Dynamic relocation is not widely used.

Allocation of storage space to segmented program

If a program is written as a number of separately compiled segments, then the linkage editor must bind these segments together. The user can specify which segments are required in store at the same time. Some segments will not be required until the processing of other segments has been completed. These segments are mutually exclusive and can occupy the same area of store. The storage requirements of the program can be expressed as a tree structure.

Segments on different branches are mutually exclusive, whereas segments on the same branch are required at the same time. For example:

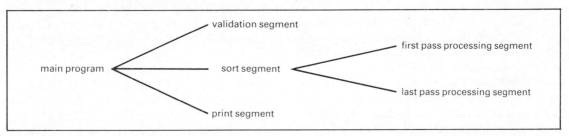

From a knowledge of the size of each segment, the maximum storage requirements of the program can be calculated. This will be equivalent to the largest branch of the tree.

There are three approaches to allocating store to a segmented program:

1 One approach is to allocate the maximum amount of store required by a program as a single contiguous block. This store is allocated to the program for the duration of the run.
2 The second approach is to allocate the full storage requirements to a program when it is loaded as two or more areas of store. The number of areas that can be allocated depends upon the number of base/limit register pairs.
3 The third approach is to dynamically allocate storage space to segments as and when each segment is required. This approach minimizes the storage requirements of the program, but can lead to an increased overhead of disk

transfers. The problem with allocating memory on demand is that sufficient free space may not be available when it is required. This means that another segment must be selected and copied on to backing store in order to make space for the incoming segment. The segment must vacate an area of store large enough to accommodate the new segment.

Allocation of storage space in paged memory systems

When a program attempts to access a location in a page that is not currently resident in store, this generates a page fault. The page containing the location must be brought into store. If an empty page frame exists then the page can be loaded directly. If all the page frames are occupied then one of the pages already present must be replaced.

The fact that pages and page frames are of fixed sizes means that there is no problem with finding a page frame of the right size. The choice of which page is to be replaced is made by a page replacement algorithm.

Page replacement policies

If one of the pages already in store is to be selected for replacement then the perfect choice would be to select a page that will not be required again. However, the future use of a page is not known and so an attempt must be made to predict which page will not be required again.

Page replacement algorithms may be local or global policies. A local policy is one that selects the page to be replaced from among the program's own pages currently in store. A global policy may select for replacement any page in store, regardless of which program it belongs to.

The number of page faults generated by a program will depend on the number of pages of the program that are in store at any one time. If the number of pages in store is increased, the number of page faults will be reduced (if the entire program is held in store, there will be no page faults). If the number of pages in store is reduced, the number of page faults will increase. During any short period, a program will refer frequently to a particular set of pages. This set of pages is known as the working set. Over a longer period the pages forming the working set will change. The current working set can be determined by considering which pages have been referred to recently. If a page has been referenced recently it is quite likely that it will be required again soon. As stated earlier, programs tend to execute instructions in loops. Therefore, a page replacement policy should not select a page for replacement that forms part of a program's current working set.

If the current working set of pages of a program is not in store, then the number of page faults will increase significantly. If there are several programs in store, none of which has its working set in store, then 'thrashing' can occur. This happens when the processor spends more time transferring pages between backing store and main store than it does processing instructions.

We shall now consider some of the replacement policies that have been implemented.

First in, first out   The page that has been in memory longest is replaced. This is a very simple policy to implement as it only requires a cyclic pointer. It does not take into account how frequently or how recently the page was referenced.

Least recently used   The page replaced is the page which has not been referred to for the longest period. To implement this policy literally would require either recording the time of every store access or maintaining a list of the order in which pages are referred to and dynamically resequencing the list every time a different page is referred to. If the policy is implemented in either of these ways then additional hardware will be required. To attempt to implement the policy either way

using software would slow down memory access considerably.

One approach used is to associate a 'use' bit with each page. Initially all the use bits are set to zero. The use bit associated with a page is set when the page is referenced. At the end of an appropriate time interval all the use bits are recorded. A use register (typically 8 bits) is associated with each page. The use bit for the most recent interval is shifted into the most significant bit position of the register and the previous contents of the register are shifted right; the least significant bit is lost. The binary pattern recorded in the use register shows the use of the page during the previous eight time intervals. A page that has not been referenced since the first of the last eight time intervals will have a use register with the pattern 00000001. A page that has been referenced during each of the last eight time intervals will have a use register with the pattern 11111111. These bit patterns can be treated as values.

The page with the lowest value has been used least recently and can be replaced. In the event of more than one page having the same lowest value, the page to be replaced can be selected from those with lowest use values on a first in, first out basis.

If, instead of recording the history of page use, the selection of the page to be replaced is based solely upon its use during the recent time interval then the policy becomes the 'second-chance' algorithm. Effectively the second-chance algorithm is a variation on the first in, first out policy. A cyclic pointer is again used. The page selected for replacement is the first encountered which has not been referred to during the previous time interval. Each use bit that is examined and found set will be cleared and passed over.

One simple improvement to the algorithms can be made by the use of a 'write' bit. The write bit is set if the contents of the page have been altered since it was last brought into store. The write bit indicates that the version of the page in store differs from the version held on backing store. If the page selected has not been altered while in store then it need not be copied back on to the backing store, and the version of the page in store may be overwritten.

Least frequently used The page replaced will have been referred to least during the period preceding the page fault. This method requires a count to be kept of the number of times each page is referred to. The overheads of keeping a separate count for each page are quite high. It is important that a page which has been used extensively but is now finished with should not be kept in store after it is required. Therefore, the count for each page should be reset to zero at the start of each interval. A page that has only recently been brought into store may still have a low count when the next page fault occurs. No page that has been brought in during the last interval should be selected for replacement.

Device management systems

This section considers the problems associated with allocating peripherals to a program and controlling the transfer of data to and from peripherals.

Allocating peripherals
The method of specifying the peripheral requirements of a program differs from one programming language to another. FORTRAN uses device numbers to represent peripherals within a program; COBOL and Pascal allow the user to assign file names to peripherals. The device numbers and file names are associated with a type of peripheral and not a particular device. A reference to a magnetic tape file, for example, does not specify which tape drive the tape is to be mounted on. When a peripheral is to be allocated to a program, the device management system can select any available device of the appropriate type. The program is not then dependent upon a specific device being available.

The device management system may allocate devices

When a program is loaded
When an OPEN statement is encountered, during program execution
Upon the first attempt to access the device within a program.

The choice of approach will depend upon the nature of the device and the characteristics of the programming language.

By allocating peripherals when a program is first loaded, the device management system can ensure that all the requested peripherals are available before the program is run. In order to do this, the job description must contain details of the program's peripheral requirements. Allocating peripherals when the program is first loaded has the advantage that peripheral deadlock (see below) will not occur. The disadvantage of this approach is that peripherals may be allocated to a program long before they are required. Indeed, peripherals may be specified which are not subsequently used during the execution of the program.

If the periphals are not allocated until the OPEN statement is encountered or until the first attempt to access the device, then the peripheral may not be available when it is required. As a result, the execution of the program will have to be delayed or aborted.

When a peripheral is allocated to a program it may be dedicated to that one program or shared with other programs. If a program is granted dedicated access to a peripheral, then this means that the program has exclusive use of that device. Peripherals which can only operate in serial mode must be dedicated to one program. For example, it is not possible for several programs to have simultaneous access to the line printer, because the output would not make any sense.

Dedicating a slow peripheral to one program will mean that other programs requiring that peripheral will have to wait, especially if this is the only device of its type. The concept of virtual peripherals enables this problem to be overcome. A *virtual peripheral* is a device that does not actually exist but is simulated on another device. A magnetic disk can be used, for example, to simulate several line printers. The output from the program will be held in disk files and spooled to the printer after the program has been executed.

Devices such as magentic disks may be shared. They permit several programs to access different files at the same time by interleaving peripheral transfers. The same file may be accessed by several programs if the access rights permit.

The device management system maintains tables giving details of the computer configuration (i.e. which peripherals are connected). From these tables it can determine which devices are in use, which are inoperable and which are free to be allocated. The tables also record which tapes and disks are currently mounted on the drives. When a peripheral is to be allocated, the device management system searches the tables to find a device of the correct type that is available.

If dedicated access to a peripheral is required, then a device of the correct type must be free in order to satisfy the request. A shared peripheral may already be allocated but this does not prevent it from also being allocated to another program. There is usually a limit to the number of virtual peripherals of one type that may be allocated, although this limit is often far in excess of the number likely to be required.

When a peripheral has been allocated, this fact must be recorded in the device allocation table.

Deadlock

If all the resources that a program requires are not allocated when the program is loaded, then the possibility exists that they will not be available when requested. Under these circumstances the program must wait until the resource becomes available. If a resource is held by another program which is in turn waiting for a resource held by the first program, then deadlock has occurred.

Deadlock will occur when every one of a group of programs is waiting for a resource held by one of the other programs in the group.

There are two approaches to dealing with deadlock. One method is to prevent deadlock from occurring in the first place; the second is to wait until it does occur and then attempt to recover.

Deadlock occurs when a program requests a resource held by another waiting program. It can

be prevented in one of a number of ways:

1 Ensure that all the resources required by a program are allocated when the program is loaded. This can be very wasteful of resources.
2 Do not permit a program to request new resources until it has released all the other resources that it currently holds. A program may release a resource and then immediately request it back again. This approach is of limited practical value because a dedicated peripheral, such as a line printer, may not be released if it will be required again as it could be allocated to another program.
3 Deadlock may be avoided in certain instances by withdrawing resources from waiting programs. This cannot apply to dedicated devices such as printers, but it can apply to resources which are easily recoverable such as memory space. The current contents can be saved and restored later on.
4 In order to ensure that a closed loop of waiting programs does not occur, the list of all resources is held in the order in which the resources are most likely to be required. A program can only request resources further down the list to those already allocated to the program.

The sequence in which resources are allocated to a group of programs will influence whether deadlock will occur. Consider an example using magnetic tapes as the only resource. The system has twelve tape decks, eight of which are currently allocated as shown.

Program	Tape drives allocated	Maximum number of tape drives required
P1	4	10
P2	2	3
P3	2	9

If we allocate a further tape drive to program P2 then this program is in a position to complete its processing. When program P2 finishes it will release sufficient tape drives to allow program P1 to finish, and subsequently program P3 can be completed. If, however, we had allocated the four free tape drives to either program P1 or program P3 then none of the programs would be in a position to complete their processing.

One way of avoiding deadlock is to check before allocating any resource that a sequence still exists in which all the programs can be allocated the resources they require. In order to achieve this, the maximum number of peripherals of each type required by a program must be known in advance.

If the system does not take steps to prevent deadlock from occurring then the system must detect deadlock when it occurs and take steps to recover. The algorithm used to detect whether deadlock has occurred is very similar to the algorithm used to determine whether deadlock will occur if a particular resource request is granted. In order to detect that deadlock has occurred, the system must maintain detailed information about the current allocation of peripherals and outstanding allocation requests.

When it has been determined that deadlock has occurred, the system must attempt to recover. This may be achieved by withdrawing resources from a waiting program, but a more common approach is to abort one of the waiting programs. If it becomes necessary to abort a program then the program must be selected with care. The following factors will affect the selection of the program to be aborted:

How much processing has already been performed by the program
How many resources the program already has allocated and how few more it requires
How easy it will be to 'roll back' and recover if this program is aborted
The priority of the program.

It is important that the same program should not be continually selected. In order to avoid this, it is possible to include whether the program has been previously selected as a factor for subsequent selection.

The same approach to deadlock does not need to be employed for all system resources. For example, memory may be pre-empted as its content is easily recoverable, whereas peripheral deadlock should be prevented.

Deallocating peripherals
A peripheral can be deallocated either when an appropriate CLOSE statement is encountered or at the end of the run. Many programmers collect all OPEN statements together at the beginning of the program and CLOSE all devices as the last action of the program. If all devices are closed as the last action of the program then there is no difference between the user closing the devices and the system closing the devices when the run ends.

There is a tendency in modern programming languages not to have OPEN and CLOSE statements; this is in recognition of the fact that practically all input and output is to shared or virtual peripherals. Consequently there is no disadvantage in allocating devices for the duration of a run.

There is an advantage to be obtained from deallocating dedicated peripherals as soon as they are finished with, so that they can be allocated to another program. Programming languages which include OPEN and CLOSE statements permit the programmer to CLOSE a file but retain allocation of the peripheral. This usually applies to magnetic tape devices where the file may need to be subsequently reopened.

Deallocation of a peripheral simply involves removing all the links set up in the device allocation table. When a dedicated peripheral is released, the job scheduler will be called to see if another program waiting for this device can now be run.

Peripheral connections

Device control unit
A peripheral device can be thought of as having two parts – the electromechanical part which reads and writes data, and the control unit which

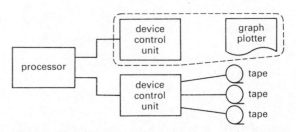

Figure 18   *Device control units*

transmits to or receives the data from the computer. The control unit may be an integral part of the device, in which case there is no need to distinguish between the two (Figure 18).

However, several devices of the same type may be connected to a single device control unit; for example, several magnetic tape units may be controlled by the same device control unit (Figure 18). The control unit is then responsible for transmitting/receiving data to or from the appropriate device. Only one of the devices may be transmitting or receiving data at a time, although other devices attached to the control unit may be performing actions which do not directly involve the transfer of data such as rewinding a magnetic tape or positioning disk heads. The device control unit may include certain error detection facilities such as parity checking on magnetic surface recording devices.

Channel processor

Device control units are not connected directly to the central processor. There are two main reasons for this:

> The difference in operating speed between the processor and the peripherals
> The great variation in operating characteristics of different types of peripheral.

Instead, the device control units (DCUs) are connected to channel processors (Figure 19). The channel processors may have their own buffers in which to store the information being transmitted to or from the devices. The contents of a channel processor's buffer may be transferred to the main store in one store access cycle by a process known as 'cycle stealing'. (In cycle stealing, the channel

processor uses one cycle of store access that would have been used by the central processor and makes use of the central processor's store access registers.) Similarly, the contents of the channel processor's buffer may be filled in one cycle. Alternatively, the channel processor may access the main store directly using its own store access registers.

Channel processors may be of two types:

> *Selector*   Several devices may be connected to the channel processor but only one may be transmitting or receiving at a time. Fast peripherals, such as magnetic disks, will be connected to selector channel processors.
> *Multiplexor*   Several slow devices may be connected to the channel processor and operate simultaneously (see sections on multiplexors in Chapter 8).
> *Block multiplexor*   Several fast devices may be connected to the channel processor and operate simultaneously by interleaving the blocks of data.

Selecting paths

Each device is connected to one or more device control units, and each device control unit is connected to one or more channel processors. The computer may have several channel processors. The computer system may be configured as a hierarchical structure, as shown in Figure 20.

In this example there is only one possible path to each device. If the channel processor or device control unit on the path to a device is inoperable, then the device cannot be used.

If the system has a configuration like the one in Figure 19, then there is more than one path to some of the devices. In this case any available path

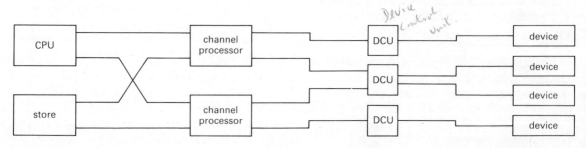

Figure 19   *Channel processor*

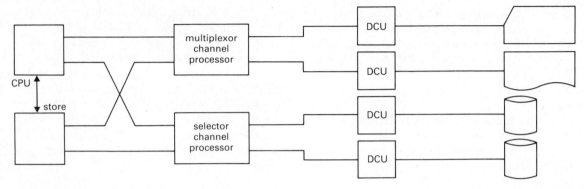

Figure 20   *Path selection*

can be selected. The path is selected for each input/output operation.

Peripheral transfers

Before a peripheral transfer can take place, the input/output management system must check the validity of the request. Some checks will have been made at compile time, such as detecting an attempt to read from a line printer. The validity of many operations, however, depends upon the sequence in which they are performed: for example, attempting to write to a file before it has been opened or attempting to read from a file past the end of file marker. The input/output management system must check the validity of all peripheral transfer requests at run time.

Reading from a serial device such as a card reader does not require a sophisticated addressing mechanism. A sequential 'read' will fetch the next physical card from the input hopper. Reading from a disk file requires that the input/output management system takes into account the way in which blocks of the file are allocated. The address of the next block to be accessed can be obtained from the previous block or an index (see 'Allocation of storage space to files' in Chapter 4).

The system selects the path to the peripheral and passes all the information necessary to perform the instruction to the appropriate channel processor. While the channel processor carries out the peripheral transfer, the central processor is free to execute other instructions.

The information passed to the channel proces-

sor by the operating system in order for it to carry out an instruction includes

1. *The device identification*   Several devices will be attached to the channel processor, so the operating system must identify the peripheral involved in the transfer.
2. *The device control unit* to which the device is attached (if the device may be attached to more than one device control unit).
3. *The operation required*   This will usually involve a data transfer but it could be a request to rewind a tape or search for a file header.
4. *The direction of transfer*   On a magnetic tape or disk the transfer of data could be in either direction.
5. *Store addresses*   The address of the first main storage locations involved in the data transfer.
6. *The amount of data* to be transferred.
7. *Disk address*   Where the data are being read from or written to a disk, the disk address (cylinder and track nos.) must be supplied.
8. *A reply word*   Used to indicate whether the operation was successful. If the operation is unsuccessful then the reply word will contain an indication of what went wrong, for example, the line printer has run out of paper.

The device management system obtains most of the information it requires from tables. As well as the device allocation table, the system will maintain tables that record the allocation of device control units and channel processors. The program will have a table for each file that is to be accessed (this table is called the file definition table). From these tables and the program instruction, the device management system can build up the information required by the channel processor.

Blocking

The unit of data specified by a read or write instruction may be a character, field or record. The unit of data transferred between peripherals and the store corresponds to the physical characteristics of the device. The physical charac-

teristics of a virtual peripheral could be different to that of the peripheral being simulated. For example, the unit of data may be a block, of say 512 characters, rather than a card image. As a consequence the first read instruction may result in a block of data being transferred. This may be more than is necessary for the read instruction. Not all subsequent read instructions will actually result in a data transfer between peripheral and store; some transfers will be between storage locations.

Exercises

3.1 Why is allocating storage space to whole programs inefficient?

3.2 Why would it not be possible to convert program addresses into memory addresses when the program is loaded?

3.3 What is the difference between segmentation and paging?

3.4 (a) How are program addresses converted into memory addresses using a base register?
   (b) What is the purpose of the limit register?

(c) Figure 21 represents a memory map showing the programs currently resident in memory. Consider the following sequence of events:

1 Program E size 4K enters job queue.
2 Program F size 4K enters job queue.
3 Program G size 5K enters job queue.
4 Program H size 14K enters job queue.
5 Program D finishes and releases its store.

Describe the effect that the following placement policies would have upon the sequence of events above:

(i) First-fit
(ii) Best-fit
(iii) Worst-fit.

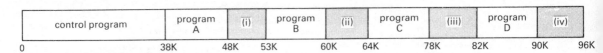

control program	program A	(i)	program B	(ii)	program C	(iii)	program D	(iv)

0   38K   48K   53K   60K   64K   78K   82K   90K   96K

Figure 21 *Memory map for Exercise 3.4(c)*

3.5 A memory with sixteen page frames has been allocated to three programs. The distribution of the page frames is as follows:

Program	X	X	Y	Y	Y	X	Z	X	Z	Z	X	X	X	Y	Z	Z
Page no.	8	9	7	6	3	3	4	2	1	2	1	4	16	1	5	6
Use register (4 bits)	0111	1000	0011	1111	0011	1110	0100	0010	0011	0111	1100	0001	0101	1010	1101	1100
Page frame no.	0	1	2	3	4	5	6	7	8	9	10	11	12	13	14	15
Use bit	1	1	0	1	0	1	1	0	1	0	1	0	0	1	1	0
Write bit	0	0	1	1	0	1	0	1	1	1	1	0	0	0	0	0

If a local least-recently-used page replacement policy is used, which page would be selected for replacement if a page fault occurred in

(a) Program X
(b) Program Y
(c) Program Z?

If the following reference counts are associated with each page frame, which pages would be selected by a local least-frequently-used policy?

526 618 24 48 100 72 1024 168
1100 1524 248 68 841 56 928 724

3.6 What is meant by

(a) Virtual peripherals
(b) Shared peripherals
(c) Dedicated peripherals?

How does the peripheral type affect the allocation of the peripherals?

3.7 What information is required by the device management system in order to execute a peripheral transfer instruction?

3.8 Why does a program read or write statement not always result in a peripheral transfer?

3.9 Why does storage lockout take place when a peripheral transfer is executed?

3.10 How can the storage lockout for a read instruction differ from that of a write statement?

4 File management systems

Introduction

On early batch computer systems, each user was responsible for his own file management. Creating a new file involved specifying where on the storage device the file was to be placed. No restrictions were imposed upon other users who wished to access the file, except through data control. The user was also responsible for ensuring that copies of his files were taken at regular intervals.

With the advent of multi-access computer systems, the user became physically remote from the computer. Such systems permit users to access files from a distance, but without restrictions users would be free to access any file regardless of the sensitivity or privacy of its contents. These restrictions of access must be provided by a file management system. A file management system can also be used to enable a user to consider only the logical characteristics of a file, that is, to view a file as a sequence of records. A user would prefer to ignore the physical aspects of file handling, such as allocating file space, the positioning of records and taking back-up copies of the files. Although file management software was originally developed for multi-access computer systems, its use is equally applicable to other types of system.

The important functions provided by a file management system are:

1 To provide a simple mechanism for creating and accessing files
2 To provide a facility for editing the contents of a file
3 To protect files against unauthorized access
4 To protect files from hardware malfunction.

The description of file management systems falls into four main categories:

1 The identification of files and control of access
2 The allocation of storage space to files
3 The back-up system for preserving the integrity of the stored information
4 Editing the contents of files.

Identification of files and control of access

File identification
Each user is assigned a unique user name, which is used to identify that user to the system. When the user logs into the system he types in his user name and password. He may have the impression that he is the only user. If he asks for all the current files to be listed, only his own files will be catalogued. This is because the file system maintains a file directory for each user. The fact that each user has his own directory helps to preserve the impression that he has exclusive access to the computer. He may access any of the files listed in his directory.

Two-level file stores
In a two-level file store the user name is used as the key to search a master file directory to identify the user's file directory. The file name can then be used to locate the file required by searching through the user's file directory (Figure 22).

The master file directory contains an entry for each user. Each entry will comprise

The user's unique name
A password to permit access to the user's file directory
The location of the user's file directory (the user file directory is itself a file, and like any other file will be held on a backing storage device)
Accounting information recording the use made of the system.

The user file directory contains an entry for each of the user's files. Each entry in the user file

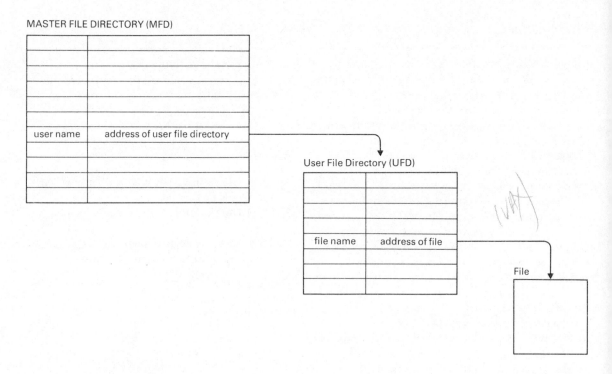

MASTER FILE DIRECTORY (MFD)

user name	address of user file directory

User File Directory (UFD)

file name	address of file

File

Figure 22   *Two-level file store structure*

directory may contain:

The file name   The file name need not be unique, as there can be different versions of the file. The file name can be qualified by a file type or generation number. The combination of file name, file type and generation number must be unique within the directory. The same file name can be used by different users.

The file type   This gives an indication of the nature of the contents of the file; for example, BIN for a binary file or TXT for a text file.

The generation number   The generation number is used to distinguish between different versions of a file. Each time a file is updated a new version of the file is created with a different generation number. Previous versions of the file can consequently be retained.

The cartridge number of the disk containing the file.

File access restrictions, indicating who may access the file and what functions they may perform.

The file size

The file organization, e.g. serial, sequential, direct, indexed.

Information to enable security copies of the file to be taken automatically and, if necessary, to locate the security copy. To provide an automatic file back-up facility the directory will record whether the file has been altered since the last security copy was taken. Security copies are usually held on magnetic tape and can be located from the serial number or increment number of the tape. See section on protection of files, later in this chapter.

Hierarchical file stores

The directory structure described above is known as a two-level directory structure and is used by many file management systems. More sophisti-

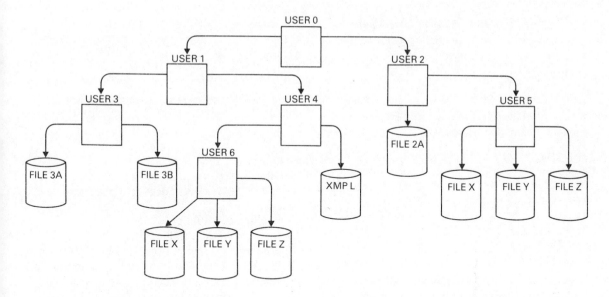

Figure 23   *Hierarchical file store structure*

cated file systems make provision for each entry in a user file directory to point to either a file or another user file directory. This enables hierarchical file directory structure to be created. This tree structure, shown in Figure 23, enables better organization of the files. A user can subdivide his files according to the application.

One of the best known of the early hierarchical file systems was the file store of ICL's GEORGE III operating system. Many modern operating systems, such as UNIX, also offer a hierarchical file directory structure.

Each user file directory must be identified by a unique user name. This user name is usually allocated by a 'super user'. (The super user is a system user with special privileges, usually the systems manager or systems programmer. The terminology differs from system to system; super user is the term used by UNIX). The user name is used to identify the directory which will be used as the working directory when a user logs on. It is usually accompanied by a password to ensure that the user has the authority to use the name. A file directory is itself a file and is represented by a single entry in its parent directory in the same way as any other file. The file directory must have a

name by which it is identified in the parent directory. In many systems this name need not be the same name as the user name, although to use two different names to identify the same file can lead to confusion. In many systems the user name is identified by a unique prefix; for example, /USER2 in UNIX or :USER2 in GEORGE III.

A user is not restricted to accessing only the files in his own file directory. Providing the user has been granted the right of access, he may access any file in the system as long as he can identify the file (access rights are covered below).

The best way to illustrate the different methods of accessing files that do not belong to a user's working directory is to illustrate the approaches of GEORGE III and UNIX.

One way in which a user may refer to a file in another directory is to change his working directory to that of the parent directory of the file. He can change his working directory by means of a change directory command. For example, to change the working directory to USER4:

CD/USER4 (UNIX)

or

DIRECTORY :USER4 (GEORGE III)

The user will be required to know the appropriate password, and then he may refer to any of the files owned by this directory.

In GEORGE III's file store a file may be referred to by its absolute name. The absolute name of a file comprises the user name of the directory which owns the file coupled with the file name; for example,

USER4.XMPL

A user can also access any file further down the same branch of the tree by specifying a path to the file from a user file directory for which he has access rights; for example,

USER6.FILEX

The UNIX operating system does not provide facilities for referring to a file by its absolute name, but the user may specify a path to any file from either his own file directory or the root directory. The path may ascend the tree as well as descend the tree in order to reach the required file. Each of the directories on the path will be prefixed by either '..' to indicate a parent directory or '/' to indicate a child directory. If the path is to start with the root directory then this is indicated by starting the file path with a '/'. The file name will be prefixed by a full stop. For example, to refer to the file XMPL from directory USER3, either of the paths

/USER0/USER1/USER4.XMPL

or

..USER1/USER4.XMPL

may be used.

Linking files
It is possible to set up a link from one user's directory to another user's file. This link must be set up by the owner of the file. The user whose directory now contains the link does not become the new owner but may have been granted special access privileges. The user may refer to the file in the same way as he would any other file in his directory, by simply specifying the file name.

Aliasing
It is possible in many systems for a user to equate a frequently used path with an alias. For example,

PROG = /USER0/USER1/USER4.XMPL

The file XMPL may now be referred to simply as PROG.

Such links can usually only be set up for the duration of a terminal session. To avoid having to establish these links every time the user logs on, they may be written into a macro command to be obeyed as the first event of every terminal session.

Controlling the right of access to files
Under certain circumstances it is necessary to allow a number of users to access a file, but there is a need to restrict what they may do with the file. For example, all users should be able to use the Pascal compiler but they should not be able to make modifications to it. As another example, casual users should not be permitted to amend the payroll file, but the personnel department will need to add or delete records and the accounts department will need to update the salaries. Obviously there is a need to distinguish between different categories of user and perhaps to grant each category different access privileges.

Categories of user may be described as

The owner
Privileged users
General users.

The owner
Several file directories may contain an entry for a file, but only one directory may contain an entry indicating that the user is the owner of a file. Other users' file directories may contain an entry for the file set up as a link by the owner. The owner may determine who can access his files and what access rights they are entitled to. Ownership of a file can be transferred. For example, a program under development will belong to a project team or programmer until the program becomes operational; then the ownership can be transferred to the user department's file directory.

Privileged users
Groups of users or individual users can be granted

access rights different from those granted to the general user or the owner of the file. These users must be identified to the system. Two ways of identifying the users are:

User groups   Each user is a member of a group, and any other member of the same group can access the user's file with the special privileges granted to the group by the user. During a terminal session a user may change groups in order to access files belonging to another group. To do this he will need to know the password.
Partners   The owner of a file may explicitly state lists of other users who can be granted access. This list may apply to a directory and consequently all the files within the directory. Different individual users can be granted different rights of access.

General user
Any user who does not fall into one of the categories above is restricted to the access rights granted to the general user.

Access privileges
Each category of user may be granted different access privileges. These may range from no access at all to the right to alter or even delete the contents of a file. The type of privileges that may be granted are:

N   *No access* at all.
E   *Execute* only (this only applies to object code files).
R   *Read* only: the contents of a file may be listed or used as data to be input to a program.

A   *Append*: records may be appended to the end of a file but the existing records may not be altered.
W   *Write*: allows the user to alter the contents of a file.
D   *Delete* a file.

In some systems the access categories are considered as different levels of access. The granting of one level of access implies all the levels above that level. In other systems each access category granted must be explicitly stated.

It is advisable that the owner of a file should not grant 'delete' status even to himself. If he wishes to delete the file he should first change his own right of access to delete status and then delete the file. This avoids the file being deleted inadvertently. Usually, only the owner of a file or a 'super user' can change the access rights.

Separating logical and physical storage structures
The file system must show the logical relationships between files and their owners as well as the physical relationship between the files and the storage devices. Some systems separate the two relationships. In UNIX, for example, the hierarchical file system depicts only the logical relationship between files and their owners. A directory entry will contain only the file name and a pointer to the physical file storage structure, called the inode (see below). There is one inode for each file; it contains the location of the file, access rights, size and organization of the file as well as relevant data about the owner of the file and the date and time that the file was last modified.

Allocation of storage space to files

File space on magnetic disks is allocated in fixed-size blocks. The files, however, are variable in length and so a policy for allocating storage space to files is required. Only a few policies for allocating storage space are available to choose from.

Contiguous blocks
The file is allocated contiguous blocks of disk storage space. This system was used on the IBM 1130, but it has many faults. The system does not permit records to be appended to a file without creating a new file area. The system leads to

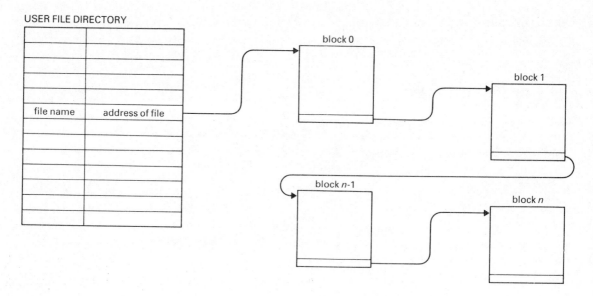

Figure 24   *Linked blocks*

fragmentation of the disk space. When a copy of a file is deleted it is very unlikely that the storage space released will be exactly the same size as any other file, which will lead to small fragmented areas of disk space being wasted. The user file directory entry for a file will point to the first block of the file.

Linked blocks

The blocks allocated to a file may be allocated anywhere on the disk and chained together. The user file directory points to the first block in the chain and each block points to the next in turn (Figure 24).

The only form of access to the file is sequential as blocks can only be reached by working along the chain. The free blocks are also chained together. Files can be updated *in situ* by linking in extra blocks and by deleting existing blocks. When a block or a file is deleted, it is returned to the chain of available free space. Extending or deleting the file can be made easier by including a pointer in the user file directory to the last block of the file.

Indexed blocks

In the two methods of organizing file space described above, the blocks must be scanned sequentially, which makes them unsuitable for files which are to be accessed in any other way. In order to be able to access blocks at random the address of each block must be held in an index (Figure 25).

The address of the index is held in the user file directory. To locate a particular record it is necessary to calculate which block contains the record. The algorithm used to identify the block will depend upon the file organization. The address of the block can be found from the index.

In the case of very large files, more than one index may be necessary. Index blocks can be chained together to create one big single-level index but most systems use two or more levels of index.

The UNIX file system uses up to four levels of index blocks. The first-level index is referred to as an inode and contains thirteen entries. The first ten of these entries point to blocks of the file; the remaining three entries point to indirect index blocks.

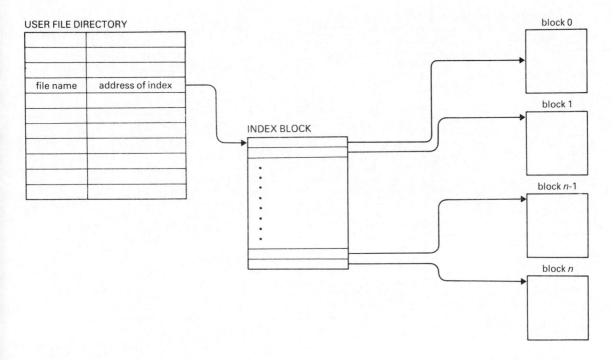

USER FILE DIRECTORY

file name	address of index

INDEX BLOCK

block 0

block 1

block *n*-1

block *n*

Figure 25 *Indexed blocks*

The principle of the system is that it is only necessary to increase the level of indirection as the size of the file increases. The larger a file, the greater the number of indexes that are required (Figure 26).

The inode block points directly to the first ten data blocks of the file. A file that contains no more than ten blocks requires no second-level index. The eleventh entry points to a second-level index block, which points to a further 128 data blocks. If the file is larger than 138 data blocks then a third level of indexing is necessary. The twelfth entry in the inode block points to a third-level index, which in turn points to 128 more second-level index blocks. The final entry in the inode block points to a fourth-level index, which in turn points to 128 more third-level index blocks. The total potential file capacity using all levels of indexing in this way is over 1 billion bytes. However, the greater the number of levels of index, the more disk transfers are necessary to locate a single record.

Protection of files against software and hardware malfunction

The contents of a file may be lost or corrupted at any time. The file may be corrupted by an error in the software or lost owing to a hardware malfunction. A failure in the middle of updating a file could cause both the old and new copies of the file to be lost. The only satisfactory way of ensuring that the contents of a file are not completely lost is to make a copy. Security copies

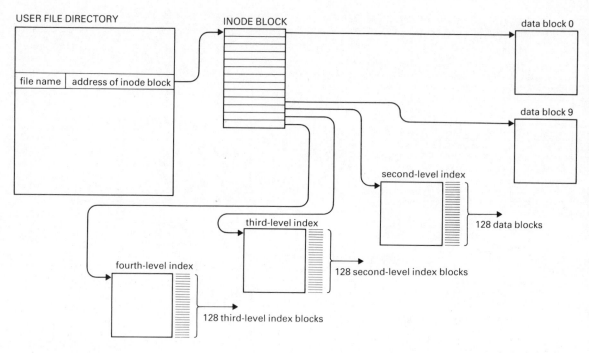

Figure 26   *Indirect index blocks*

must be taken at reasonably frequent intervals and held on a different disk or tape to the original version of the file.

The interval between taking copies of files should not be too long as the data contained within the back-up copy may well be out of date by the time it is required. The interval between taking file copies should not be too frequent, either, as copying files makes considerable demand upon the computer's resources. If the computer system has limited resources then no other functions can be performed while file copying is taking place. It is important to remember that copies of the file directories should be taken as well as copies of the files, because if the complete file system should be lost the directory structure must be rebuilt.

There are two approaches to taking security copies of the file store. The first approach is to take a complete copy of the file store. The second is to perform a selective copy of only the files and directories that have been updated since the last copy was taken.

To take a complete copy of the file store can be very time consuming and usually requires that the system is devoted entirely to the copying process, at least for part of the time. The complete file store can be copied either by starting at the master directory and working down the tree, copying each file and directory in turn, or by making duplicates of each disk. These copies may be taken on either disk or tape. If the copies are made on another disk rather than tape, then the process will not take as long.

If complete copies of the file store are taken, then in the event of a system failure the file store can be easily recovered. Duplicate volumes can simply replace any damaged or corrupted disks. If the file store is copied on to tape, then retrieving an individual file can take a considerable time. The file store will occupy several different physical tapes, which have to be searched to locate the file required.

Selective copying, usually called *incremental dumping*, takes less time than copying the complete file store. The GEORGE III file store

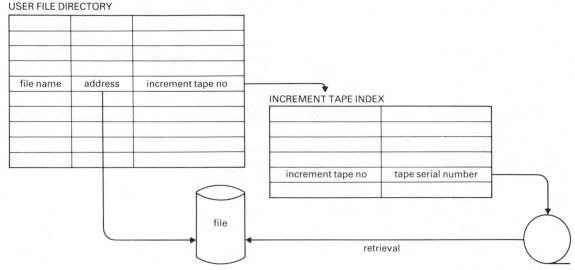

USER FILE DIRECTORY

file name	address	increment tape no

INCREMENT TAPE INDEX

increment tape no	tape serial number

file

retrieval

Figure 27 *Incremental dumping*

introduced incremental dumping to take copies of the file store. At periodic intervals, determined by the system manager, all files and directories that have been created or updated during the period between dumps are copied on to an increment tape. To further improve security, the copies may be made simultaneously on to two or even three tapes. The increment tapes will contain a complete copy of the file store, but it will be spread over a number of tapes. The files on some of the earlier increment tapes will have been subsequently updated and more recent copies taken. A tape-to-tape processor routine can be run to consolidate the information upon the increment tapes. A new set of tapes is created which contains only the latest copy of each file and directory.

If incremental dumping is used then each directory entry contains the increment number of the tape holding the back-up copy. The increment tape number is a logical number and the increment tape index relates this to the tape serial number of the physical tape(s) containing the file copies. When an increment dump is taken, the increment may occupy several physical tapes. After a tape-to-tape processor has processed the early increment tapes, several increments may be contained on one physical tape. See Figure 27.

In the event of a system failure, the file store

must be recovered. This requires loading the latest copy of the master file directory and, from the information within this directory, loading the directories and files of the first level down the tree. From these directories the next level of the file store tree can be rebuilt. It is unlikely that the file store will be completely rebuilt. It is more likely that the general restore routine will be designed to retrieve just sufficient directories and files for the file system to become operational, and then further files will be retrieved individually as they are required. Rebuilding the complete file system can take a considerable time.

To retrieve an individual file, the number of the increment tape containing the file copy is obtained from the directory. The serial number of the physical tape containing the file can be obtained from the increment tape index. The back-up copy of the file can then be retrieved from the tape. The retrieval of an individual file does not take long.

Recovery
It may be necessary to invoke a recovery procedure for a number of reasons, such as hardware or software failure or because deadlock has occurred.

The extent to which a file system must provide

recovery facilities is dependent upon several factors:

  The nature of the system, i.e. batch or on-line
  The level to which an organization is dependent upon the system
  The frequency with which files are updated
  The extent to which files are updated on-line.

A short-running batch program could be aborted and rerun, but for longer-running batch programs and on-line programs it may be necessary to adopt more satisfactory recovery procedures. At periodic intervals a copy will be taken of all the files relating to a program. This can be used as the basis for a subsequent recovery. All transactions applied to the files will be recorded on a journal file. This file is usually referred to as the *transaction log*. At intervals a marker will be placed on the transaction log to indicate a point to which the system can return without errors. The transaction log usually contains copies of all transaction records as well as copies of the updated records. The copies of the updated records may be taken before they are updated (before images) or after the records are updated (after images).

In the event of an error occurring, it will be possible to recover the files to the point immediately prior to the failure, either by 'rolling back' or by 'rolling forward'.

Roll back   The transaction log is used to 'undo' the transactions that caused the error. Records updated since the last marker are replaced by the before-image records copied from the transaction log.

Roll forward   In this case the system works forward from the last complete dump. The files are re-established from the dump copies and updated by copying the logged after-image records. The transactions up to the most recent marker can be reapplied.

Editing the contents of a file

File editing is only performed on data, text or source files, i.e. character files. The organization of these files is serial or sequential. Three types of file editor are generally available:

  Line editors
  Text editors
  Screen editors.

Line editors   ICL 2904.
Line editors use line numbers as the key to identify the records to be edited. The operations that can be performed by a line editor are restricted to:

  Insert a new record into its correct sequential position
  Delete a single record or block of records from the file
  Replace one or more records by another record or block of records.

The order in which the records are edited must correspond with the order of the records in the file.

In most systems, if the file does not already exist then the file editor will create a file area and an entry in the file directory. The editor will then treat all records as inserts. In some less sophisticated systems the process of creating a file area must be performed by a separate utility. Line editors are predominantly used in batch systems.

Text editors   Zenith, Condor.
Text editors operate on a different principle to line editors. Instead of altering complete records, individual characters or strings of characters may be edited. The amendments do not have to be applied in sequence, but one has to imagine a pointer that can be moved backwards or forwards through the file to identify the text to be amended. Text editors are most frequently used

on-line, in which case the user's file is transferred into a workspace or buffer for editing. The pointer can then be moved around this buffer space. It can be moved to either end of the buffer, to a particular line number, or it can be moved backwards or forwards a specified number of characters, words or lines. The pointer can also be used to locate particular passages of text.

Once the pointer has been moved to the correct position, editing can take place. Once again the three basic editing operations are

Insert new text
Delete a specific passage of text
Replace one passage of text by another.

When one passage of text is replaced by another then the passages need not be the same length. Several occurrences of the passage may be replaced at the same time. Every occurrence of the passage or a specified number of occurrences of it from the current pointer position may be replaced. Using a text editor, a single character can be quickly located and changed.

Screen editors – VAX
Screen editors allow the user to edit the portion of the file displayed upon a visual display screen, using special function keys. The function keys enable the user to

Move the cursor around the screen
Display a different portion of the file
Delete or insert text
Move a passage of text to a different part of the file.

This type of editor operates in a similar manner to a text editor, except that instead of manipulating an imaginary pointer the user moves the cursor around the screen. Individual function keys (usually identified by arrows) enable the user to move the cursor to any character position on the screen.

The screen image can be changed by 'rolling' the screen image backwards or forwards through the file or by skipping to another portion of the file. Particular function keys will move the cursor to the beginning or end of the file. Alternatively, the cursor can be moved to the beginning of a particular passage of text.

When a user has moved the cursor to the required position on the screen, he can then insert or delete text. The function keys enable the user to delete the character, word or line of text indicated by the cursor. When text is deleted from the screen it is held in a buffer. The contents of the buffer can be replaced in the file. This facility to replace the contents of the buffer can be used to move a word or line of text from one part of the file to another, or to make several copies of the same word or line of text. Text input from the keyboard will be inserted into the file in the position indicated by the cursor.

Larger passages of text can be moved using 'cut-and-paste' techniques. Separate function keys will be used to select the start and end of a passage of text to be cut from the file and to indicate where it is to be inserted or 'pasted' into the file. The same passage of text may be pasted into several different positions in the file.

Exercises

4.1 What are the basic functions of a file management system?

4.2 What information about each file will be contained in a file directory entry?

4.3 How may USER6 in Figure 23 refer to the file named FILE3B which belongs to

USER3 and to FILEZ belonging to USER5?

4.4 What access privileges would you grant for each category of user to the following files?

(a) Student record file. The college registrar is responsible for students enrolling on courses and the lecturing staff will wish to record the students' grades for course assessment and examinations.

(b)   Employee payroll file. The personnel manager is responsible for recruitment of staff and the company accountant is responsible for determining rates of pay.

(c)   A COBOL compiler.

(d)   A sort work file.

4.5   Decide upon a suitable policy for taking security copies of students' programs and data files on a college's mainframe computer system.

4.6   Compare the facilities provided by the text editor described in the chapter with the editor provided on a computer system to which you have access.

5 The development of programming languages

The earliest computers were programmed using plugboards or by setting switches on the computer's console. There were no programming languages as such; all programming was done 'physically'. The first development was to write programs in machine code which were held on paper tape. Each instruction would be read in as it was required. By joining the two ends of a paper tape together to form a loop a sequence of instructions could be executed more than once, hence the term 'programming loop'. Conditional execution of instructions was achieved by selecting which of several paper tape readers was to be used to read the next instruction.

When the concept of storing programs in the computer's memory was introduced, mnemonic codes were developed to overcome the difficulties of programming computers at the machine level. Mnemonic function codes were used to represent operations and symbolic names could be used instead of actual storage locations. Whole programs could be written using mnemonic codes and input to the computer on punched cards or paper tape. These mnemonic codes were the first primitive assembly languages and considerable effort was required on the part of the programmer to overcome their limitations. Assembly languages are thought of as 'low-level' languages.

The first development towards simplifying the programming task was the introduction of 'automatic programming' systems. These provided an assembly-level language with a range of instructions which were not provided by the machine itself, such as floating-point arithmetic and simplified input/output commands.

The next stage in program development was to provide programming languages which permitted algebraic expressions to be input. The most significant of these early algebraic languages was FORTRAN; developed by IBM in the late 1950s. It is still in wide use today, although originally nobody envisaged that it would be used outside

IBM. (The word FORTRAN is an acronyn for FORmula TRANslation.)

A large number of programming languages rapidly followed. Some languages were developed to solve a particular type of problem, whereas others were intended as general purpose languages. However, by the nature of their instruction sets and the range of facilities they offer, all programming languages are more suitable for some problem areas than others. These languages are known as 'high-level' programming languages because they are problem oriented and not machine oriented.

The traditional high-level programming languages, such as COBOL, FORTRAN, Pascal and BASIC are procedural languages. That is, they provide the user with a basic set of instructions which enable him to specify how a procedure is to be performed. By contrast, non-procedural languages permit the user to state 'what' he wants without having to specify 'how' it is to be achieved.

Non-procedural languages are used to develop systems in specific application areas, such as

> Report generating programs
> Database enquiry systems
> Input validation programs
> Defining and updating files and databases
> Management systems.

Non-procedural languages are sometimes known as fourth-generation languages.

For each language a piece of software is required to translate a program into a code that the computer can understand. For a high-level programming language this piece of software is usually known as a compiler, for a low-level language an assembler, and for non-procedural languages a generator.

This chapter describes different types of language processing software and the stages that a program goes through while being translated into machine code. Figure 28 is intended to illustrate the purpose of these language processors.

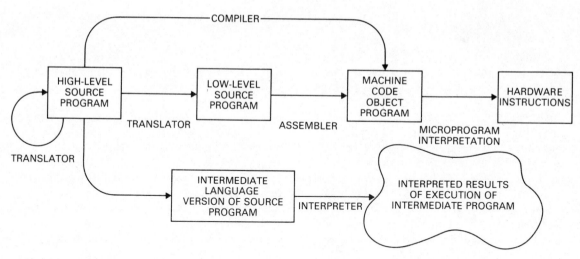

Figure 28 *Types of language processor*

Types of language processor

Assemblers

Each computer system has its own low-level programming language, which is designed to exploit the particular feature of the machine. Each instruction of a low-level program corresponds closely with a machine code instruction. The low-level programming instructions have a fixed format, which is generally of the form

    label   :   function   :   operands

The function is a mnemonic indicating the action required and usually represents one machine code instruction. However, many low-level languages make use of macro instructions which when translated generate several machine code instructions.

Instructions generally have two operands. The operands may be references to registers or to storage locations. Most low-level language instructions operate upon a register; they can be register-to-register instructions, register-to-store instructions or store-to-store instructions. The computer may have one or several registers that the programmer can access. A number or letter code is used to represent the register. A storage location is usually referred to by a symbolic name, although it may be referred to indirectly (indirect addressing), in which case the location referred to by the symbolic name contains the address of the actual location required. A storage location may be referred to by its absolute program address (direct addressing) or as a displacement relative to the position of the instruction being executed (relative addressing). Instead of specifying a storage location, one of the operands may be a literal value. The use of a literal value as an operand is sometimes referred to as immediate addressing. Some instructions require no operands at all.

The process of translating a low-level program into a machine code object program is termed 'assembly' and is performed by an assembler. An assembler is a fairly straightforward piece of software. The process of translation consists of two operations. The function code must be converted into machine code and the labels and storage locations referred to by symbolic names must be translated into program addresses. In some languages the function code will correspond to more than one machine code instruction. The selection of the correct machine code instruction will be based upon the addressing technique used.

Like the early 'automatic programming' systems, the machine code instruction set provided does not necessarily exactly match the instruction set of the hardware. The hardware is programmed with a microprogram which dictates the characteristics of the machine code. By changing the microprogram the characteristics of the machine code can be altered. Conversely, alterations to the microprogram can be made to avoid changing the machine code when hardware changes are made. (Not all computers are microprogrammed. On some computer systems all functions are provided by hardware; for example, Amdahl 470 computers.)

Microprogramming has been used to provide ranges of computers with the same low-level programming language. Instructions that are provided by hardware units on the larger faster machines can be simulated on the smaller, slower computers by microprograms. Consequently the same assembler is applicable to several different machines.

Compilers

A program that is written in a high-level language will be converted into machine code by a compiler. The version of the program that is input to the compiler is called the source program, and the compiled version of the program is called the object program. A compiler which just performs the task of translating a program from source code into object code is sometimes referred to as a 'true' compiler. This is to distinguish it from compilers which place special emphasis on one particular aspect of the process such as improving run-time error messages or producing highly efficient object code.

Diagnostic compilers

During the development stages of a project, when programs are being tested, the programmer requires that run-time error messages should be as meaningful as possible. Diagnostic compilers are designed for just this purpose.

To produce meaningful error messages entails incorporating a considerable amount of extra code into the object program. The compiled program must retain references to the original variable names, and to the original source lines that contained the code. Then when an error occurs

the error message printed out can relate to the original source code that generated the error.

Meaningful error messages enable errors to be detected and corrected much faster than if the user has to rely upon the sort of information normally provided by the operating system. Typically this is a simple code or message indicating a group of possible error conditions and an object program address indicating where the error was discovered. It is often very difficult to relate this type of information to the original source program.

Optimizing compilers

The object code produced by a compiler must be correct but it is not necessarily efficient. Certainly if the code is produced by a diagnostic compiler it will be far from efficient. Optimizing compilers are designed to produce more efficient code. The level of optimization will vary from compiler to compiler and from language to language (see below). Even some diagnostic compilers incorporate a degree of optimization, but at the highest level of optimization even the sequence in which instructions are executed may be changed.

Although the code produced by an optimizing compiler is often very efficient, it must be remembered that the use of an optimizing compiler cannot compensate for the choice of the wrong algorithm. For example, the choice of an inefficient sorting technique cannot be overcome by an optimizing compiler.

The use of an optimizing compiler should be reserved for fully tested programs. This is not only because it is difficult to diagnose errors that occur in an optimized program but also because of the considerable overheads involved in using an optimizing compiler. An optimizing compiler uses more processor time than other types of compiler.

Incremental compilers

Incremental compilers are designed for interactive use at a terminal. An incremental compiler does not process complete programs but performs a line-by-line compilation. Each program statement input from the terminal is translated immediately. Any error messages relating to the statement can then be printed out on the next line. This gives the user opportunity to correct one line before typing in the next. Many versions of BASIC are implemented using incremental compilers.

Because the compiler translates one line at a time it is not capable of detecting all the possible errors. This means that errors which are not detected at compile time must be left until run time. Consider the following examples:

1   Suppose that the first line of a BASIC program typed in by a user is

     30 LET X = Y(12) + 1

     The statement refers to an array Y which has not been given dimensions. The element referred to as yet has no value. These facts cannot be reported as errors at this stage because the user may later type in the lines

     10 DIM Y(15)
     20 LET Y(12) = 0

2   Suppose that the user has already typed in the three lines above and now types in the line

     10 LET Z = 1

     This line has the same line number as a line already input. This means that as well as compiling the new line the compilation of the previous line must be 'undone'. This is called backtracking and is a considerable problem for the compiler writer.

Translators

Not all language processors produce machine code. One example of a processor for which the object code is not machine code is a translator. The purpose of a translator is to produce as output a program equivalent to the one input but in a different language. The translation may be from a high-level language into a low-level language or from one high-level language into another. The object code can then be translated into machine code using the assembler or compiler appropriate to the object program.

Translating a program from a high-level language into a low-level language was a technique used in the early days of computing in order to make high-level languages available quickly. A translator can be produced with relatively little effort, and although the two-stage process of translation and assembly is time consuming it does allow programs to be written in a high-level language while an appropriate compiler is written.

A second use of the translator is to convert a source program written in a language that is no longer supported on a particular machine into one that is. For example, when ICL introduced the 2900 series they ceased to support NICOL, a programming language available on the 1900 series. They did, however, make available a translator to convert NICOL programs into COBOL.

Interpreters

An interpreter differs from other language processors in that it does not generate an object program. The eventual output from a compiler is an object program which can be loaded into the appropriate machine to be executed under operating system control only. An interpreter, however, will simulate the execution of the source program.

An interpreter has two stages

1   The conversion of the source program into an internal code. (This internal representation is often achieved using reverse Polish notation: see below.)
2   The interpretation of the internal code to simulate the execution of the program.

The two stages of the interpreter may be performed separately, in which case the entire program is converted into an internal form before actual interpretation begins. Alternatively the two parts may be integrated, in which case each instruction is translated immediately before it is required to be executed. When the two stages are performed separately then each instruction need be translated only once, but when the two stages are integrated each instruction is translated every time it is to be obeyed.

The internal code is usually held in what is called a 'source retrievable form'. This means that if an error occurs during the interpretation of the program then an error message referring to the original source text can be printed out.

Programs written in certain languages, such as APL and LISP, cannot be compiled but must be interpreted; this is because some statements remain ambiguous until run time. Compilers for a subset of these languages are often available.

Application program generators

The term 'application program generator' is used to describe a software tool that assists in the development of application programs as an alternative to the conventional procedural high-level programming languages. Application program generators are non-procedural in their approach.

One of the essential features of application program generators is that the development of systems should be user friendly. The techniques used to develop programs using these products reflect the popularity of interactive terminal-based systems. Many of the systems assume that the user is working at a visual display unit and utilize this fact by displaying prompts for the user. These prompts may take several different forms. They may be a series of questions to which the user supplies answers (usually yes or no) or they may be a list of options (menu) from which the user selects using the cursor key. Alternatively the user may start with a blank screen and use the cursor and keyboard to develop the layout of the screen. This technique of 'screen painting' is used to prepare screen formats for the input or output of data. The code necessary to display the eventual screen image and to handle any associated input data will be generated automatically.

The other common method of developing an application program using a generator is to input a sequence of commands which are used in much the same way as the instructions of a programming language. The commands, however, are used to specify what is required and ignore the more procedural aspects of how it is to be achieved. Languages of any type have the disadvantage for the lay user that he must learn the syntax of the language. This is a disadvantage of the command languages that is not apparent with the screen-based methods.

Application program generators may be of two types:

Code generators   The output produced is in the form of a high-level procedural language source program which can be subsequently compiled or interpreted by the appropriate translator for the high-level language.

Application generators   These do not generate an output code but produce an internal version of the program which is interpreted by the application generator.

Cross-compilers and cross-assemblers

The object code produced by a compiler is usually intended to be run on the same machine as the compiler. If a compiler produces object code which is to be run on a different machine it is called a cross-compiler. Likewise, an assembler that produces code to be run on a different machine is called a cross-assembler. Cross-compilers and cross-assemblers are often used to produce code for processors which are too small to support a compiler or assembler.

Compiler construction

A compiler can be written as a number of separate routines, each routine being responsible for one stage of the compilation process. The entire source program can then be processed by each routine in turn. Alternatively, the compiler can be written as a single routine which takes one statement at a time and translates that directly into object code.

When a program is processed by each of the routines which performs one or more of the stages of translation, this is called a 'pass'. The first approach mentioned above describes a multipass compiler, and the second approach describes a single-pass compiler.

Not all programming languages are suitable for translation by a single-pass compiler. An instruction can only be compiled directly from source code into object code if all of the details of the instruction are known in advance. This means that all variables must be declared before they are used. No compiler can, strictly speaking, be a single-pass compiler, as this would eliminate the use of forward branches. These must be satisfied by a short second pass. A single-pass compiler eliminates the need for an internal intermediate version of the program.

Stages of a multipass compiler

The phases of a multipass compiler can be broadly grouped together into two stages

The first stage involves the analysis of the source program statements and the building of an internal representation of the program. Each program statement must be identified and checked to see that it conforms to the permissible syntax for that statement. Every programming language has rules of syntax which govern the format of instructions. The compiler must first identify which instruction the programmer has used and then examine whether the instruction has been correctly used.

The output from the first stage of the compiler will be an internal representation of the program held in the form of tables. The most important of these is the intermediate code table and the symbol table.

The second stage of the compilation process is the translation of the program from its internal representation into object code. Figure 29 shows the stages of translation in more detail.

Lexical analysis

Programs are written as lines of source code and input to the compiler from a physical medium such as magnetic disk or a terminal. Each input record represents a line of source text but not necessarily a program statement. The syntactic and semantic analysis routines of the compiler are concerned with the structure and grammer of

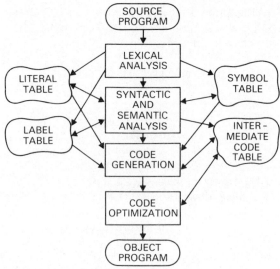

Figure 29   *Stages of compilation*

program statements. The writers of these routines prefer to ignore the external characteristics of the input records and treat each program statement as a string of 'tokens'.

Consider the statement

A := B − C;

This statement is made up of the tokens
    A, :=, B, −, C, ;.

The lexical analysis routine will input the lines of source text and pass basic statement 'tokens' to the syntactic and semantic analysis routines. The routine will remove any particular characteristics of the input medium from the lines of source text. The tokens system will cope with records that are split over more than one line. Records will often have redundant spaces at the end and these will be removed during lexical analysis. In the same way the return character at the end of each line input via a terminal will be removed.

Program statements are constructed from two different types of token. The tokens can be standard symbols of the programming language such as 'begin', := and ;, or user-defined symbols such as data names and literals. Program comments are ignored by the lexical analyser. The lexical analysis routine will represent each token by a code. Standard symbols can be represented by a single byte, but user-defined symbols must have one byte indicating the type of symbol (i.e. literal, data name or file name) plus a pointer to the entry for the symbol in the symbol table. The lexical analysis routine is often described as a separate stage that precedes the syntactic and semantic analysis stage. In practice the lexical analysis routine will be written as a subroutine (or number of subroutines) called by the syntactic and semantic analysis routines.

Syntactic and semantic analysis

The syntax of a programming language is a set of rules dictating how the basic program elements are ordered to form statements. Syntactic analysis is the process of analysing the format of each statement in order to identify the instructions and to verify that they are grammatically correct.

For example, if the format of an instruction is specified as

ADD dataname-1   dataname-2
   GIVING   dataname-3

then the instruction can be recognized by the keyword ADD. The instruction

ADD I J GIVING K

is syntactically correct. However, the instruction

ADD I AND J GIVING K

does not conform with the syntax specified, so is incorrect.

The syntax analysis is performed by a routine called 'the parser' and the process is referred to as parsing. The semantic analyser checks that each instruction written is valid. For example, although the instruction

ADD I J GIVING K

is syntactically correct, it is only valid if the variables I, J and K are of compatible types. The instruction would be semantically incorrect if any of the variables were declared as character type.

The syntactic and semantic analysis can be performed in separate stages but it is much more likely that the semantic analysis process will be built into the parser.

Parsing routines

The parsing routine accepts as input the tokens produced by the lexical analyser and from these builds what is called a 'parse tree'. The tree need not actually exist; it may only be built in the figurative sense. Examples of a program and a program statement represented as tree structures are shown in Figure 30.

The tree need only exist to the extent that the parsing process works through the program as though it were constructing a tree in order to

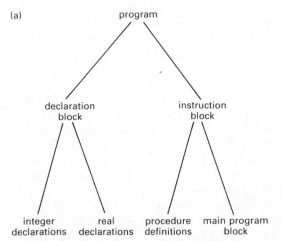

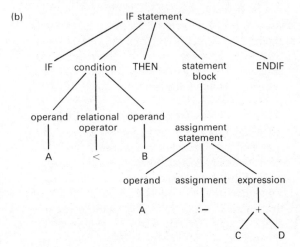

Figure 30   *(a) Parse tree for program structure*
(b) Parse tree for IF statement

analyse the syntax. The output from the parser will be an internal representation of the program.

Parsers may build trees from the top-down or from the bottom-up.

Top-down parsers   The top-down approach is based upon the assumptions that the input to a parser will be a program statement. The language grammer will define the subcomponents of each statement and the parser searches for and analyses each of these subcomponents in turn. Two top-down approaches (recursive descent and LL parsing) are outlined below.

A recursive descent parser uses a set of procedures to analyse the syntax of program statements. If we consider a statement such as

IF condition THEN statement ELSE statement ENDIF

the statement procedure will identify the instruction by the keyword IF. A procedure to process the IF statement will be called. This procedure will in turn call further procedures to analyse the component parts of the statement. This will involve recursive calls upon the statement procedure. A recursive descent parser is relatively easy to write but takes a long time to analyse the statement because of the number of procedure calls involved.

A recursive descent parser represents the tree structure of a statement by the way it calls the procedures. When one of the procedures is called, the return address is held in a stack. The stack, therefore, represents the tree. The order of the statement components can be recognized from the sequence in which the procedures are called.

The approach of an LL parser is very similar to that of the recursive descent parser. An LL parser identifies a statement by its keyword and then uses a table to indicate the component parts of each statement. This table is called the parse table. The parser uses a 'look-ahead' technique when more than one alternative construction of the statement is possible. The method relies explicitly upon a stack to cope with nested statements.

Bottom-up parsers   A bottom-up parser builds up

the tree from the bottom. The approach is for the parser to look for subcomponents which it can recognize and from these attempt to identify statements. One method of bottom-up parsing is known as 'LR parsing'. An LR parser makes use of a stack. Each token output from the lexical analyser is placed upon the stack. The parser examines the elements at the top of the stack, and if it can identify a group of elements as a subcomponent then it will replace them by a single stack element identifying that subcomponent. The elements displaced are moved to the intermediate code table. The subcomponent will be used with other subcomponents and tokens to build up complete statements.

Tables

During the early stages of the compilation process an internal image of the program is built up and held in tables. The most important of these tables are the intermediate code table, which holds the internal representation of the program's instructions, and the symbol table, which keeps information about each of the labels, variables and literals used within the program.

Intermediate code tables

The internal representation of the source program is built up during the analysis stage of the compilation process. The intermediate code used to represent the internal form of the program is closer in format to machine code than to the original statements of a high-level programming language. The same internal codes are suitable for both compilers and interpreters and are portable between computer systems.

The intermediate code instructions will consist of operators and operands. The operators will not at this stage have been converted into function codes as these will depend upon the types of the operands. The operands will not as yet represent program addresses but will be pointers to entries in the symbol table.

The choice of internal representation will depend upon the language being compiled, the language the compiler is written in and the preferences of the compiler writer. The most commonly used forms of representation are

	A := B * C + D * E	D := B ** 2 − 4 * A * C
Reverse Polish	A BC * DE * + A :=	DB2 ** 4A * C * − :=
Triples	(i) * , B , C (ii) * , D , E (iii) + , (i), (ii) (iv) := , A , (iii)	(i) ** , B , 2 (ii) * , 4 , A (iii) * , (ii) , C (iv) : = , D , (iii)
Quadruples	* , B , C , T1 * , D , E , T2 + , T1 , T2 , A	** , B , 2 , T1 * , 4 , A , T2 * , T2 , C , T3 − , T1, T3, D

Figure 31 *Examples of triples, quadruples and reserve Polish notation as internal representations of code*

reverse Polish notation, quadruples and triples. A combination of these methods may be used within one compiler.

Reverse polish notation   Reverse Polish notation is often used for arithmetic and logic expressions but can be extended to include all programming language constructs. It is a method that is extremely simple to implement but is not very suitable for code optimization.

The Polish notation was devised by Professor J. Lukasciewicz of Warsaw University in the 1920s. Lukasciewicz's notation was a prefix notation which placed an operator before its associated operands. For computing purposes this notation has been reversed so that an operator succeeds its operands. Thus the reverse Polish representation of A + B becomes AB+. One of the distinct advantages of this notation is that the precedence of the operators may be maintained without using brackets. For example,

A * (B + C)   becomes   ABC+*
(A * B) + C   becomes   AB*C+

The generation of reverse Polish is based upon the use of a stack. The order of the operands within a reverse Polish string is the same as that within the original expression. The operators are added to the reverse Polish string immediately following their associated operands (see Figure 31). The operators are given a priority when they are placed upon the stack. The priority is based upon the order of precedence of the operators. The priority ensures that the operators appear in their correct position in the reverse Polish string.

Reverse Polish notation automatically generates strings in which the operators occur in the same sequence as they must be executed. The length of the reverse Polish string is dependent upon the length of the original expression; there is no fixed length for reverse Polish strings. Reverse Polish notation is a convenient alternative representation to the original arithmetic or logical expression. It is not very close in format to machine code instructions but, because the operators occur in the same sequence as they will be executed, it is a simple process to generate the object code from a reverse Polish expression.

Quadruples and triples   Quadruples and triples are much closer in format to machine code instructions than reverse Polish strings. Both quadruples and triples have a fixed format.
   Quadruples consist of four fields

operator , operand1 , operand2 , result

An instruction such as A := B + C would be represented as +, B, C, A. Where the instructions are more complex then intermediate results will have to be stored in temporary locations generated by the compiler. For example,

F := A * B + C

becomes the quadruple sequence

*, A , B, T1
+, C , T1, F

(T1 is a temporary variable.)

Triples consist of only three fields

operator   ,   operand1   ,   operand2

The result of any machine code instruction is likely to be left in a register. This fact is recognized by the triple notation. Each triple is assumed to have a value which will be left in a register by the code generated from the triple. There is, therefore, no necessity to store results at this stage in temporary locations. The number of registers, however, is limited and the code generation routine may have to make use of temporary locations to supplement the use of registers.

An expression such as

A := B + C

will generate the following triple sequence:

Triple no.	Triple
(i)	+ , B , C
(ii)	:= , A , (i)

(i) represents the result of triple no. (i).

A triple sequence for an arithmetic expression may be generated by first representing the expression as a tree. Consider the tree and triple sequence for the expression $(1 - R)/(1 - R ** N)$, shown in Figure 32.

A triple sequence can also be conveniently generated from a reverse Polish string. The advantage in doing this is that a triple sequence is more convenient for code optimization.

Symbol table
The symbol table may be generated at the same

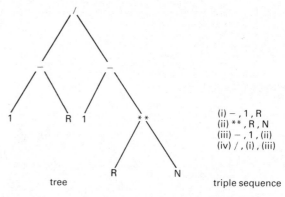

(i) − , 1 , R
(ii) ** , R , N
(iii) − , 1 , (ii)
(iv) / , (i) , (iii)

tree   triple sequence

Figure 32   *Tree and triple sequence for (1-R)/(1-R**N)*

time as the intermediate code table, but in most cases the symbol table will be built up first. In languages such as COBOL all variables must be declared at the beginning of the program. The size, type and scope, the number of dimensions and initial values of all variables are known in advance and can be used to construct the symbol table. In a language like Pascal, where both global and local variables are permissible, the symbol table must be generated at the same time as the intermediate code.

In a language such as APL even the number of dimensions of an array may change at run time. This means that the symbol table must be capable of reflecting alterations made at run time, and is one of the reasons why APL programs must be interpreted rather than compiled.

The compiler writer may choose to use separate tables for variables, constants, literals and labels declared by the user. However, better use is made of the available storage space if they are all held in a single table.

A considerable amount of information must be recorded in the symbol table about each data item. The information can be broadly identified as

Characteristics of the data item.
The information required to access a data item.

The characteristics that must be included to give a picture of each data item include:

1   The name of the item.
2   Whether the item is a scalar (a single data

item), an array, a list (in the context of linked lists), or a group item.

3 The number of dimensions if the item is an array and the upper and lower limits of each dimension (if known at compile time).

4 Whether the data item is a constant or a variable (some languages, for example Pascal, distinguish between the two).

5 The type of the data item, i.e. integer, real, character, Boolean or user-defined type.

6 The size of the item, i.e. number of characters or digits.

7 The address of the item, when storage space is allocated. This may not be known if storage space is allocated dynamically at run time, for example with linked lists.

8 Whether the item is a formal parameter to a procedure or subroutine.

The entries in the symbol table may be accessed by the compiler using one of the following techniques:

A linear search, which is time consuming.
A binary search, which requires the entries in the symbol table to be in sequence.
A hashing algorithm (see next chapter). A very careful choice of hashing function must be made to avoid the possibility of collisions.
A binary tree. The tree is searched from the root to locate a symbol.

In block structured languages where local variables may be declared, temporary symbol tables can be created. These tables are then collapsed as soon as the block containing the declarations has been compiled.

Generation of code
This is the stage that actually produces the object code. The input to this stage of the compiler will be the tables produced by the analysis stage. The machine code instructions are generated from the intermediate code with reference to the symbol table. Each operator is converted into a function code. The types of the operands will dictate the actual function code; for example, REAL variables will indicate a floating-point instruction. The operands of the intermediate code are

pointers to symbol table entries and must be changed into addresses. Most machine code instructions operate upon the contents of a register. The code generation routine must ensure that the register used in an instruction contains the value of one of the operands. The value may be placed in the register by a load instruction or left in the register as the result of a previous instruction.

Operand address
It is not always possible to calculate the address of a storage element at compile time. If the size of an array is not declared until run time, then the code necessary to calculate the address must be incorporated into the object program. As the accessing of array elements often occurs many times within a program, the calculation may be performed by a subroutine. The calculation of array element addresses is a prime area for optimization.

Register allocation
One approach to the problem of register allocation is to assume that there is an unlimited supply of registers when generating the code and then to map the imaginary registers assumed to exist on to the set of real registers available. Inevitably the number of registers available will be fewer than the number required. In this case storage locations must be used temporarily to hold the contents of some of the registers. Careful selection of which register contents to hold in temporary locations will minimize the number of load and store operations necessary.

Registers are used for several different purposes: to hold the return addresses for subroutine calls, for arithmetic computations, for base addresses and for stack pointers. One very general approach to the problem of register allocation is to reserve groups of registers for specific functions.

Code optimization
The term 'code optimization' covers a wide variety of techniques for improving the object code produced by a compiler. The purpose of these transformations will be to produce either

More efficient object code, i.e. a program that executes faster, or
Smaller object programs

Code optimization is, perhaps, not the correct term to use, as not all of the techniques can be guaranteed to produce the best possible code. A term such as 'code improvement' would be more appropriate, but code optimization has become universally accepted.

Some of the code optimizing techniques may be applied while the object code is being generated. Others may be applied as a separate stage after the object code has been produced. Not all optimizing compilers achieve the same degree of optimization. Optimizing compilers can be classified according to the extent to which they transform the object code. The extent of the optimization may be restricted to

1 *Simple statements*   The component parts of a statement such as array subscripts, arithmetic or Boolean expressions, but not assignments.
2 *A basic block*   Eliminating common subexpressions and evaluating sequences of statements with operands of known value. (A basic block is a section containing no labels, no branches and no optionally executed code.)
3 *Whole program*   Program loops and further subexpression elimination.

The aspects of programming languages which are particularly suitable for optimization are as follows;

Arithmetic expressions
There are a number of ways in which the code generated for arithmetic expressions can be considered for optimization:

1 Functions called with a constant argument can be evaluated by the compiler rather than the program. For example, if a program includes the function call SQRT(17) then the compiler can call the SQRT function, evaluate the result and incorporate the value within the object code.
2 Expressions involving known constants can often be partially if not wholly calculated in advance. Consider the sequence of statements

PI := 3.1415926;
CIRC := 2 * PI *RADIUS;

This can be reduced to

CIRC := 6.2831852 * RADIUS;

3 An operator can be replaced by one which executes faster:

Multiplication and division by powers of two can be reduced to arithmetic shift instructions.
Division can be reduced to multiplication by the reciprocal of the divisor.

Array subscripts
If the subscripts of an array are constants and the dimensions of the array are known, then the address of a particular element can be calculated at compile time. Even if only some of the subscripts are constants the calculations may be reduced.

Boolean expressions
Logical expressions can be optimized using short-circuiting techniques. For example, as soon as one relation in the expression

$$(A = B) \text{ OR } (C = D) \text{ OR } (E = F)$$

has been evaluated as true there is no necessity to evaluate the subsequent relations.

Eliminating common subexpressions
If part of an arithmetic expression has been calculated previously and the result is still available, then this subexpression need not be re-evaluated.

Consider the sequence

A := B * C;
B := B * C;
C := B * C;

The first two calculations of B * C produce the same result. This can be recognized; the code produced will be equivalent to

A := B * C;
B := A;
C := B * C;

However, C := B * C; cannot be optimized as the value of B has now changed.

Loops

One of the most profitable areas for optimization is program loops. This is because every change, no matter how small, is magnified by the number of times the loop is performed. Loop transformations fall into two categories:

Those relating to the construction of a loop
Those which move loop-invariant expressions out of a loop.

Although a program loop is a convenient way for a programmer to specify that a number of instructions are to be executed more than once, a loop actually increases the number of instructions that are executed. One way of improving the execution speed is for the compiler to unroll the loop.

For example, the statement

```
FOR I := 1 TO 5 DO
        A [I] := 0;
```

takes longer to execute than the sequence

```
A [1] := 0;
A [2] := 0;
A [3] := 0;
A [4] := 0;
A [5] := 0;
```

because of the necessary loop control instructions.

Considerable savings may be achieved by moving expressions which do not change their value during the execution of the loop, out of the main body of a loop. Such expressions are said to be loop invariant. For example, the calculation of C/D in the section of code

```
FOR I := 1 TO 100 DO
BEGIN WRITE (A[I]);
        A[I] := A[I] + C/D;
END
```

is performed every time the loop is executed. The calculation is loop invariant and can be moved outside the loop with the result that it will be performed only once:

```
t1 := C/D;
FOR I := 1 TO 100 DO
BEGIN
WRITE (A[I]);
A[I] := A[I] + t1;
END
```

Great care must be taken in identifying and moving loop-invariant expressions. If in the above example D = 0 then the author of the original code would be very confused by a divide error occurring before any results are written.

Linkage editors

Many of the functions performed by a program, such as accessing a file, will not usually result in complete object code being generated by the compiler. Instead the compiler will generate a call to a library subroutine. This subroutine will be incorporated into the program during a separate stage after the compilation has been completed. This stage is known by many different names, the most commonly accepted of which is 'linkage editing'.

The call reference to a subroutine will not be satisfied by the compiler. The compiler places the subroutine name into an external symbol table, which is stored with the compiled version of the program.

The precompiled subroutines are held in library files. The more commonly used routines such as the file access routines will be held in a standard systems library. There may also be specialist libraries containing, for example, graphics routines or statistical functions. Users may also create their own libraries of subroutines for particular applications. (These routines must be held in compiled form.)

The linkage editor will take each unsatisfied reference from the external symbol table and search the library files. The standard systems library file will be scanned automatically, but any other library files to be searched must be specified by the user.

The subroutines referenced may include further references to other subroutines. It is quite permissible to call one subroutine from within another. Therefore, each subroutine within the library file will have its own external symbol table. These references must also be satisfied by the linkage editor. The editor will scan the libraries for each reference in the subroutine's external symbol table.

The linkage editor can also be used to specify the destination of the completed object program. The object code may be left in store to be run immediately or, more usually, placed in an object code file from which it can be retrieved later for execution.

Exercises

5.1 What is the difference between a compiler and an interpreter?

5.2 How does an incremental compiler differ from other compilers?

5.3 What is the difference between a single-pass compiler and a multipass compiler?

5.4 What particular feature of programming languages makes a true single-pass compiler impossible?

5.5 What is the purpose of the lexical analysis stage of a compiler?

5.6 Draw a parse tree for the following assignment statements:

$$Y := A * X**2 + B * X + C;$$
$$VOL := PI * R**2 * H;$$

Express the parse tree as a triple sequence.

5.7 For a program that you have written construct a symbol table as it might be built up by a compiler.

5.8 Identify how the following section of code could be optimized:

```
PI := 3.1415926
FOR R := 1 TO 10 DO
    FOR H := 1 TO 5 DO
        VOL [R, H] := PI * R**2 * H/3
```

Part Two

Databases

6   Database systems

The conventional approach to processing data is to start by designing a physical data structure, such as an indexed sequential file, to represent the data within the computer system. A program is then written to process the appropriate physical data structure. The design of the program is often hampered by the physical structure used to represent the data.

The database approach is to hold all the data in a central reservoir. This central reservoir is separately administered by a database management system which permits the user to concern himself with only the logical relationships between items of data.

The database management system (DBMS) is a software interface between the data and the users (Figure 33).

The users who may wish to access the database fall into three categories.

The database administrator

An organization that implements a centralized policy for controlling its data should appoint one person to be responsible for the contents of the database. This person is known as a database administrator and is responsible for defining the structure of the data within the database. In practice the database adminstrator may be the leader of a team of people responsible for the contents of the database. The description of the contents of a database is generally called the schema, and the database administrator uses a data definition language (DDL) to create or alter the schema.

The responsibilities of the database adminstrator can be summarized as

(a)   To define the data elements. The database administrator does not define the values of the data but specifies the size and type of the data elements.
(b)   To define the relationships between data elements.
(c)   To define the security requirements of the database.

(d)   To ensure that the contents of the database are consistent and that the database contains as little redundant information as possible.

The structure of the data will affect the performance of any programs attempting to access the data. The database administrator is, therefore, responsible for the performance of programs which access the database. The performance of an application program is dependent upon the design of the database as well as the design of the program. It is less costly to rectify faults in the design of a program than those in the database.

The applications programmer

He will require access to portions of the database from within his programs. The subset of the database as viewed by the programmer is described by a subschema. He may wish to insert, alter or delete items of information within the database. This can be achieved by incorporating data manipulation language commands within his program.

The on-line user

He will wish to access the contents of the database from a terminal. On-line enquiries may be made using a query language. This is a special form of data manipulation language designed to access a database from a terminal. It enables the user to manipulate the contents of the database, in much the same way as from within a program, but by typing in individual commands from the terminal.

Some database management systems do not support a query language. In such cases on-line enquiries are made by incorporating data manipulation language statements in a host program which has terminal handling capabilities.

On-line operation should be reserved for enquiries which result in small volumes of output, and should not be used as a method of obtaining lengthy reports.

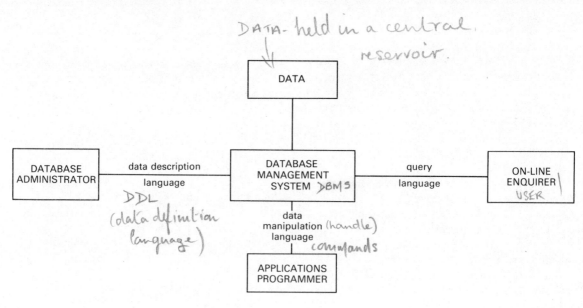

Figure 33   *Database management system*

Database philosophy

The concept of a database incorporates the idea that all of an organization's data is held as a single large collection of information that can be accessed by any of the organization's systems, though an organization may have several different databases. The data should instantly reflect any changes made. If one program updates the information held within the database then it will be immediately available to other programs. It is no longer necessary to pass files from program to program.

A company has a very large investment in the information used to run its organization. Information is a very important asset in today's society and companies must take steps to protect their investment. The information held in a database must be protected against unauthorized access and against hardware or software malfunction. The company will wish to protect its data from outside organizations; there will also be sensitive data to which the company's executives and managers will not wish their employees to have access.

In the event of a hardware failure the system must take steps to recover the lost data. This requires taking frequent back-up copies and logging all transactions. The cost of taking the necessary steps to protect data or to recover from a hardware failure should be measured against the cost to the organization if the information were to be lost.

The user will access the information within the database by incorporating data manipulation language commands within his application program written in an established language such as COBOL or FORTRAN, or by using a query language. The database approach protects the user from any concern about the physical characteristics of the storage medium. The user is shielded from any changes made to the structure of the data and need only concern himself with the logical relationship between the items of data. These relationships can reflect their natural relationship within the organization. The use of a database enables real savings in programming time and costs to be made when developing new applications. The time taken and cost of maintaining existing applications is also considerably reduced.

By adopting a centralized approach to the storage of data, several particular advantages may be gained.

Non-redundancy

In a conventional file-based system, each program may have its own copy of the data. The same field may physically occur in several different files. Maintaining multiple copies of the same information is wasteful of storage space, and a central repository for data reduces the necessity to keep multiple copies of the same item. Although only one physical copy of a field may be kept it can appear in several different logical database files. To keep only a single copy of a field may result in requirements for extra indexes and pointers in order to access the items of data.

Indexes are useful for retrieving individual items, but if the data items are being retrieved in sequence using indexes then access may be slowed. Therefore, it may not always be desirable to eliminate redundancy.

Consistency

If there is more than one copy of the same data element then the possibility exists that one copy could be altered while the other copies are left unchanged, thus leading to an inconsistency in the data. The DBMS can be used to ensure that the data remains consistent. If only one copy of a data element is held within the database then the possibility of inconsistency does not arise. If more than one copy of a data element is held it is still possible to control inconsistency. The solution is for the system to be made aware that multiple copies exist and to ensure that they are all updated (see 'Data dictionaries' later in this chapter). By permitting the user to string together several commands which cannot be interrupted it is possible to ensure that no other user can access a data element until all copies have been updated.

Data independence

The view of the data presented to the user is independent of the physical storage structure used to represent the data internally. Most application programs are written in a manner which is dependent upon the way in which the data is structured. The user of a database system may write his programs independently of the way in which the data is physically stored. The program is dependent only upon the user's logical view of the data. The user's view of a data item is independent of how the field is represented. For example, a field held as a binary value can be viewed by the user as a decimal field.

Database architecture

The architecture of a database system can be broadly divided into three levels, generally referred to as the external, conceptual and internal levels. The external level gives the user's view (of which there may be several) of the database. The conceptual level gives the logical view of the complete database, and the internal level gives the physical view of the complete database (Figure 34).

The description of the database as viewed by a user is called a subschema. The logical view of the complete database is described by the schema.

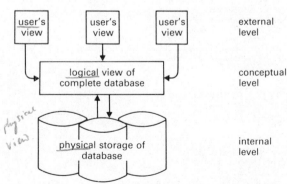

Figure 34 *Database architecture*

Creation of a database

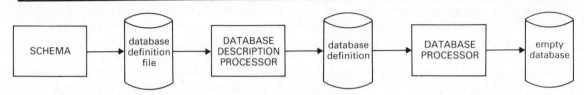

Figure 35   *Creation of a database*

One of the functions of a database administrator is to create the database. The conceptual view of the

(a)

```
 1  SCHEMA NAME IS TIMETABLES-DATABASE
 2
 3  RECORD NAME IS LECTURERS
 4   DUPLICATES ARE NOT ALLOWED FOR LEC-NAME.
 5   02  LEC-NAME   PIC X(30).
 6   02  LEC-GRADE   PIC X(4).
 7   02  SALARY   PIC 9(5) V99.
 8
 9  RECORD NAME IS DEPARTMENT
10   DUPLICATES ARE NOT ALLOWED FOR DEPT-NO.
11   02  DEPT-NO   PIC 99.
12   02  DEPT-NAME   PIC X(30).
13
14  RECORD NAME IS COURSES.
15   02  COURSE-NO   PIC 99999.
16   02  COURSE-TITLE   PIC X(30).
17   02  COURSE-TUTOR   PIC X(30).
18
19  RECORD NAME IS TIMETABLE.
20   02  DAY   PIC 9.
21   02  PERIOD   PIC 99.
22   02  SUBJECT   PIC X(20).
23   02  ROOM   PIC X(4).
24
25
26  SET NAME IS STAFF
27   OWNER IS DEPARTMENT
28   MEMBER IS LECTURERS
29   LINKED TO OWNER
30   INSERTION IS AUTOMATIC
31   RETENTION IS OPTIONAL.
32
33  SET NAME IS COURSE-LIST
34   OWNER IS DEPARTMENT
35   MEMBER IS COURSES
36   INSERTION IS MANUAL
37   RETENTION IS OPTIONAL
38   SET SELECTION IS BY DEPT-NO IN DEPARTMENT.
39  SET NAME IS COURSES-TIMETABLE
40   OWNER IS COURSES
41   MEMBER IS TIMETABLE
42   LINKED TO OWNER
43   INSERTION IS MANUAL
44   RETENTION IS OPTIONAL
45   SORT-KEY IS ASCENDING DAY, PERIOD IN TIMETABLE
46   SET SELECTION IS COURSE-NO IN COURSES.
47
48  SET NAME IS LECTURERS-TIMETABLE
49   OWNER IS LECTURERS
50   MEMBER IS TIMETABLE
51   LINKED TO OWNER
52   INSERTION IS MANUAL
53   RETENTION IS OPTIONAL
54   SORT KEY IS ASCENDING DAY, PERIOD IN TIMETABLE
55   SET SELECTION IS LEC-NAME IN LECTURERS.
```

database is described by its schema (Figure 35). The schema is written using a data description language. An example of a schema for a network database is shown in Figure 36(a). The statements used to describe the database will be held in a database definition file. The normal file editing facilities of the system can be used to create and modify this description. The contents of the database definition file will form the basis of the input to a database description processor, the output from which is a description of the database in a form which the database management system can understand. The process is akin to that of compilation, in that the input to the processor is a description of the database written in terms that we can understand and the output is a description of the database which the DBMS can understand.

(b)

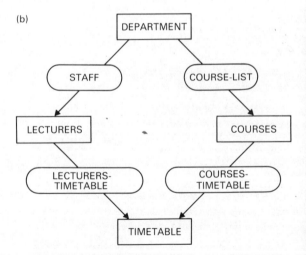

Figure 36   *(a) A sample schema for a network database (b) A data structure diagram illustrating the schema shown in (a)*

From the database description, the database itself can be created. This involves setting aside storage space to contain the database files. The database definition will have included specifica- tion of the indexes required and in some cases how the files are to be structured. Areas to contain indexes and pointers are also reserved. The empty database is now ready to receive data.

Accessing the database

The user's view
The database may be accessed by a user at a terminal, or by incorporating database commands within an application program.

The user who wishes to access the database from a terminal may be able to do so using a query language. On-line enquiries are interpreted by a query language command processor. The com- mand processor refers to the database definition in order to access data from the database. The records transferred to and from the database are stored in buffers within the command processor. The buffers can hold one occurrence of each record type. The user may access the contents of the buffers in order to display the contents on the terminal or to alter the contents before writing a new record into the database.

The user who wishes to access the database by incorporating database commands within an application program must submit his program to a preprocessor (Figure 37). This preprocessor will replace database access commands by subroutine calls. The subroutine calls and parameters will be written in the syntax of the host programming language. The program can then be compiled in the normal way. Before the program can be run the database library subroutines must be linked to the program by the linkage editor. The host program must also contain a description of that portion of the database which the user wishes to access (the subschema). The description of the subschema is normally written in the syntax of the host programming language. Some systems re- quire that the subschema is defined separately to the program, in which case the appropriate subschema is identified within the program by 'naming' it within the data declarations. Areas of storage are reserved within the program to hold

the values of items being transferred to and from the database.

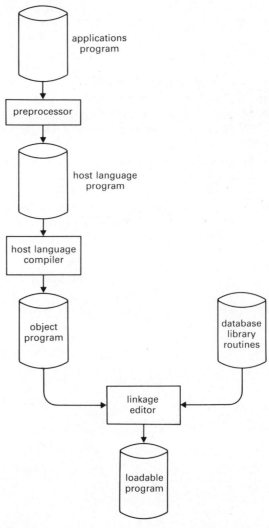

Figure 37   *User's view of accessing a database*

The system's view

When a subroutine call to access the database is encountered within an application program, this will result in the transfer of control to the database management system (Figure 38). The DBMS then uses the subschema and schema to determine whether the transfer may be permitted. It is possible on some systems to specify locks upon fields so that the contents may not be altered. Therefore, it is necessary to compare the actions required with those permissible.

If the action is permitted to proceed then the DBMS access routines are used to retrieve or store the appropriate data. The access routines must keep track of the last record retrieved in order that sequential access of records may be possible. As explained in Chapter 3, input and output to and from disks is performed in blocks of records and the necessary record may already be contained within the access routine's buffers. In this case it can be transferred directly to the program's buffer area.

The database management system may also perform transformations upon items of data. The physical representation of a field may be as a binary value, but if the subschema defines the field as a decimal number the DBMS will perform the necessary conversion.

Concurrency

Each user may have his own view of the database. This is his own logical database. However, updates performed by the user are applied to the physical database. Several different users may be accessing the physical database at the same time. When a user's program updates a database record a copy of the record is first transferred into the program's buffer area. The data values are updated in the program buffer and then the record is written back to the database. When a record is being accessed all other programs must be locked out until the record is released. This prevents the following sequence of events from occurring:

1 Program A fetches original copy of record.
2 Program B fetches original copy of record.
3 Program A writes back modified version of record.
4 Program B writes back modified version of record.

Because the two update operations overlap, the version of the record written back by program B does not take into account the modifications made by program A.

For example, a stock record may contain the following information (see next page).

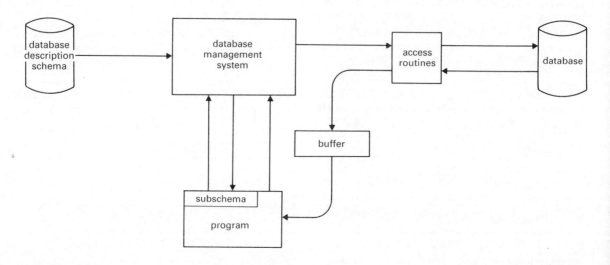

Figure 38 *System's view of accessing a database*

PART NO	ITEM	QTY
SCS1025	SCREW	75

Both programs will receive the same copy of the above record when they access the record of part number SCS1025. If program A updates the record to show that 25 screws have been received, then the record written back by program A will be

PART NO	ITEM	QTY
SCS1025	SCREW	100

However, program B is also updating the original version of the record. If program B is to record the sale of 20 screws then the version of the record written back by program B shows that 55 screws are in stock, overwriting the record written by program A rather than updating it.

PART NO	ITEM	QTY
SCS1025	SCREW	55

The type of concurrent updating problem illustrated above can be prevented by locking out any record as soon as it is accessed. Locking out single records is not always practical so entire blocks of records are locked out to ensure that the same effect is achieved.

The logical record updated by the user can comprise fields from several different physical records, which makes the process of locking out a logical record more complex. A particular problem arises if another process has already locked out the physical record containing a field to be updated.

Changing the structure of the database

It is quite likely that the structure of the database will eventually need to be changed. This may be because a new application wishes to make use of the database or because a user's view of the data has changed. Changes may involve

The addition of new fields to an existing record
The addition of new records
The addition of new indexes
Changing the description (e.g. size, type) of a field.

All programs which are affected by changes in the database structure must be recompiled.

Changing the structure of the database may require the following steps to be taken:

1 Drain all of the data out of the database into temporary storage files.
2 Make the alterations necessary to the schema; this can normally be done using the systems file editing facilities.
3 Create a new empty database from the modified schema descriptions.
4 Pour back the data from the temporary storage file into the new database.

No users may access the database while the database is being recreated in this way.

As an alternative, some database management systems incorporate facilities within the data manipulation language for dynamically restructuring the database. One such system is the IBM relational DBMS, System R. The System R data manipulation language SQL contains commands to CREATE, UPDATE or DROP tables (the rows of the tables correspond to records).

The addition of new records or indexes requires storage space to be reserved and the changes to be recorded in the database description. If fields are to be altered or added to a record then changes must be made to the physical file containing the record. One solution is to copy the contents of the file into a new file area with the changed record format. A second approach is to add a pointer field to each existing record which points to the extension to the record. (This pointer will occupy storage space itself, which is obtained by moving one of the fields of the original record into the record extension.)

A third technique is to create a parallel file in which the records are held in exactly the same sequence as the original file. The parallel file contains the fields added to the record and is addressed by the same addressing technique as the original file; only the base address of the file and the length of the records are different.

The physical view of the database

The database concept separates the logical view or user's view of the relationship between items of data from the physical view of the data, which is determined by the record and file organization. A physical file can be organized in a number of different ways, though not all of the following organizations are suitable for database files.

Serial

The position of a record within a serial file is determined by the order in which the records are written to the file. Essentially a serial file has no organization as there is no relationship between the records. The only way in which a serial file can be processed is by considering each record in turn. A serial file organization is not really suitable for database files.

Sequential

Each record within a sequential file is identified by one or more key fields. These key fields are used to define the position of a record within the file. The records are ordered on ascending or descending values of the key fields. A sequential file is processed by considering each record in sequence. This is not a very suitable file organization for database files.

Direct

The position of a record within a file is calculated by applying the values of the key fields to an arithmetic calculation. The arithmetic calculation is termed a hashing function or address generation algorithm. Records can be accessed directly by applying the hashing function to the key field values to find the address of the record.

Indexed

An index is a table containing key field values and record addresses. Individual records can be located by searching the index. The index may contain an entry for every record in a file or it may contain only one entry for a block of records, in which case the entry in the index will be for the record with the highest key value in the block.

The records within the block may be stored in key field value sequence, or the sequence of records can be obtained by chaining the records together.

The index may be organized so that the entries are held in sequential order of key field value, or a hashing algorithm may be used to locate the position of an index entry.

Both sequential files and direct files may also be accessed using an index. The index can be used to reference records using the key field or a data field.

Inverted

In a conventional file the fields of a record occupy contiguous areas of store. In an inverted file the fields of the logical record are stored in different

(a)

MODEL NO	MARQUE	ENGINE SIZE	EXTRAS PACK
1000	LADYBIRD	1.1	E
1001	LADYBIRD	1.1	L
1002	LADYBIRD	1.3	L
1003	LADYBIRD	1.3	GL
1004	LADYBIRD	1.6	GL
1005	HAWK	1.3	E
1106	HAWK	1.3	L
1007	HAWK	1.6	L
1008	HAWK	1.6	GL
1009	HAWK	2.0	GL
1010	SPEEDBIRD	1.6	E
1011	SPEEDBIRD	1.6	L
1012	SPEEDBIRD	2.0	L
1013	SPEEDBIRD	2.0	GL
1014	SPEEDBIRD	2.3	GL

(b)

MARQUE	MODEL NO
LADYBIRD	1000, 1001, 1002, 1003, 1004
HAWK	1005, 1006, 1007, 1008, 1009
SPEEDBIRD	1010, 1011, 1012, 1013, 1014

ENGINE SIZE	MODEL NO
1.1	1000, 1001
1.3	1002, 1003, 1005, 1006
1.6	1004, 1007, 1008, 1010, 1011
2.0	1009, 1012, 1013
2.3	1014

EXTRAS PACK	MODEL NO
E	1000, 1005, 1010
L	1001, 1002, 1006, 1007, 1011, 1012
GL	1003, 1004, 1008, 1009, 1013, 1014

Figure 39   (a) *Sequential cars file*
(b) *Inverted cars file*

physical records. The physical records are constructed using one data field from the logical record as the key field and the key fields of the logical record as the data fields. Figure 39 shows the same logical file represented as a sequential file and as an inverted file. The file in Figure 39(b) is a fully inverted file. Every file of the logical file record is represented by an inverted structure. It is not necessary to represent all the data fields by an inverted structure, but it is convenient to use an inverted file structure where queries of the type 'which models have engine sizes = 1·6 litres?' will be asked.

Lists
The sequential order of records within a file may be maintained by physically reorganizing the records into the desired sequence, or alternatively

by using a list file structure. A list file organization uses pointers stored within each record to indicate the sequence (Figure 40(a)).

The pointer field contains the address of the next record in sequence. Pointers can be used in both directions to enable the records to be processed in both ascending and descending order (Figure 40(b)).

By arranging that the last record points back to the first, a cyclic chain can be achieved (Figure 40(c)).

A record can contain pointers to other lists of records, thus building up linked lists to represent more complex relationships (Figure 40(d)).

Inserting and deleting records from a list file structure is extremely simple. To insert or delete a record does not require that the other records are moved. The order can be maintained by altering the list pointers.

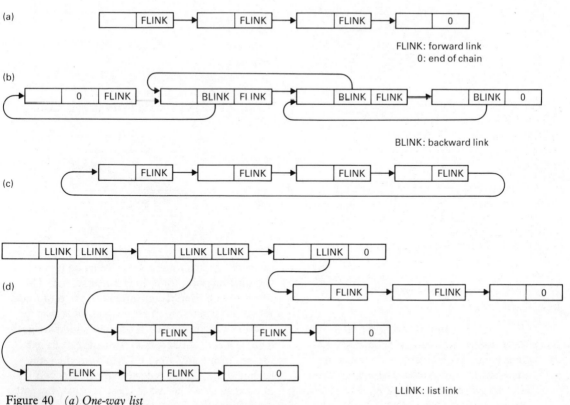

Figure 40 *(a) One-way list*
(b) Two-way list
(c) Cyclic list
(d) Linked list

Hashing functions

Hashing is a technique which subjects the primary key fields to a mathematical formula to calculate the address of a record. The file in which the records are to be placed must initially consist of sufficient empty slots to contain the number of potential records.

To calculate the address of the slot in which a record is to be placed the primary key is treated as a character string. The numeric value used to represent each character internally is multiplied by a hashing multiplier. The sum of each value calculated is accumulated and divided by the number of slots. The remainder from this calculation gives the address of the slot in which to insert, retrieve or delete the record.

The following is an example of hash addressing:

Primary key field value = LONDON

$$\text{Hash function} = \frac{(\text{sum of character codes}) \ast \text{hash multiplier}}{\text{number of slots}}$$

$$= \frac{(76 + 79 + 78 + 68 + 79 + 78) \ast 25}{53}$$

$$= 220 \text{ remainder } 40$$

(The character codes 76, 79 etc. are ASCII code values.)

Therefore the hash address is 40:

```
38 _____
39 _____
40  LONDON
41 _____
42 _____
```

Other methods for calculating the hash address have been used, such as:

(a) *Folding*   The binary string representing the primary key fields are separated into fragments. Each fragment contains the same number of bits as the hash address. The fragments are added together, ignoring overflow, to generate the hash address.

(b) *Squaring*   The binary string representing the primary key fields is multiplied by

itself. A snapshot taken from the middle of the result and equivalent in length to the hash address is used to locate the record.

When using a hashing function, it is possible that two or more keys will generate the same slot number. The possibility of a collision increases as the number of records increases. To minimize the possibility of a collision the number of records present should not be allowed to exceed abut 70% of the number of slots available. The file space should be reorganized when this figure is reached.

If a collision does occur then the new record must be placed in the next available free slot. The following is an example of a collision:

primary key field value = PARIS

$$\text{Hash function} = \frac{(\text{sum of character codes}) \ast \text{hash multiplier}}{\text{number of slots}}$$

$$= \frac{(80 + 65 + 82 + 73 + 83 + 32) \ast 25}{53}$$

$$= 195 \text{ remainder } 40$$

The hash address generated for PARIS is the same as the hash address generated for LONDON, so PARIS is placed in the next available slot

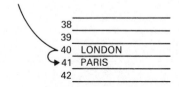

```
38 _____
39 _____
40  LONDON
41  PARIS
42 _____
```

When attempting to retrieve a record, the location given by the hashing function must be treated as the starting point for a short linear search. The linear search should continue until the required record is found or the first empty slot is reached.

When deleting a record the database management system should search forward through the file and locate any other records with the same hash address. These records will occupy contiguous stores. The last of these records should be moved into the slot vacated by the deleted record. This move will provide another empty slot and the process should be repeated.

For example, if the record identified by the primary key value LONDON is deleted then the record identified by the primary key value PARIS can be moved into its correct slot.

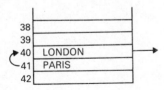

Indexing

If a field is to be accessed frequently but does not form part of the primary key then the field may be indexed. An index provides a faster method of retrieving the record. Two methods of arranging indexes are shown below.

Hashed index

Hashed indexing is the method used by RAP-PORT. A hashing algorithm is applied to the secondary key field value. This will generate a hash address for the index. Figure 41 shows an example.

B-tree indexes

The method used by System R is to organize the indexes as B-trees. A B-tree is a hierarchical index, as illustrated in Figure 42. The root node of the tree consists of three pointers and two index values. Records with a field value less than or equal to the first index value can be located by following the leftmost pointer. Records with a field value greater than or equal to the second index value can be located by following the rightmost pointer. This leaves records with a field value inside the range specified; these can be located by following the central pointer. Nodes at the lower levels operate in the same way. The terminal pointers of the tree point to an index block which is searched using a linear search. By following the appropriate pointers the block containing the required field value can be located.

Inserting and deleting records can eventually cause the B-tree to become unbalanced. An unbalanced B-tree is one in which the number of levels along each branch is different. Indexing speeds up the retrieval of records, but the indexes themselves occupy extra storage space and every

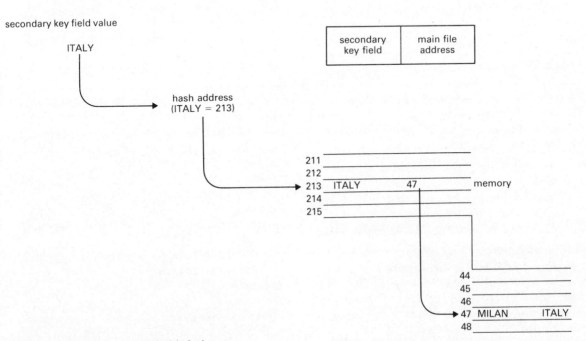

Figure 41   *Example of hashed indexing*

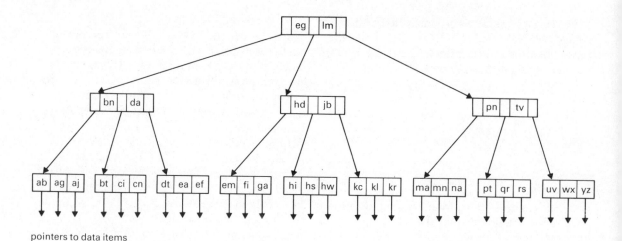

pointers to data items

Figure 42   *Example of a B-tree index*

time a record is inserted or deleted the index must be updated.

The process of locating a record using an index is invisible to the user of the database. Beyond specifying which fields have an index, the user is not aware that an index is being used, except perhaps by an improved response time.

Data dictionaries

A data dictionary is a system for providing information about the data and is itself a database. The data dictionary systems currently available enable the user to record

> Descriptions of the data fields used in the database
> The relationships between items of data
> Definitions of schema and subschema
> Details of the processes which use the data.

The data dictionary can be used by the database adminstrator to help ensure that the contents of a database are consistent and contain a minimum amount of redundant information. The user can use the data dictionary to find out what data is held in the database, and on some systems he can use the data dictionary to provide schema and subschema descriptions for inclusion within his program.

If a user proposes to change the description of a data item, then other users who access the same item must be consulted. Details of which processes access a particular item can be obtained from the data dictionary. The database administrator must decide whether to make the change or create a new data item. If more than one copy of a data item is held in the database, the data dictionary can be used to show the relationship between the two and ensure that if one item is updated then similar changes are also made to the other item.

Not all database systems use a data dictionary; nor is the use of data dictionaries restricted to database systems.

Database management systems for micro-computers

The environment in which a database management system for a microcomputer is likely to be used is very different from that of a database system on a mainframe. The purchaser of a microcomputer system is more likely to be the proprietor of a small business or a home computer user. The mainframe computer system will probably be supported by a team of database specialists, whereas the microcomputer user frequently has little previous experience of computing and has to rely upon the dealer support and database documentation. Ease of use, therefore, is an important consideration for the lonely user of a microcomputer database. Relational databases tend to be more popular with non-professional users because they are easier to understand and use.

The restrictions on database systems for microcomputers are primarily the obvious ones of processor speed and storage capacity. The time between a user requesting an item of data and that item being displayed upon the screen is the most important performance characteristic as far as the user is concerned. This access time will depend upon factors such as the speed of the processor, the choice of disks (hard or floppy) and the accessing algorithm used by the database management system. The storage capacity of the disks attached to a microcomputer is considerably less than the storage capacity of a mainframe, and consequently the DBMS may impose limitations upon the user. The user may find restrictions upon the number of fields/bytes per record, the number of records or the number of files that he may define in the database. The use of either an 8–bit or a 16–bit processor will impose limitations upon the size and accuracy of numeric data fields.

There may also be limitations upon the available data types.

The techniques for specifying the layout of the screen for input or output or the format for printed output can vary from system to system. The first microcomputer database systems mirrored their counterparts on the larger mainframes and used established programming languages or specially developed command languages/menu systems to define the input and output formats. More recent systems have exploited the characteristics of the microcomputer and its visual display unit. These systems present the user with a blank screen which he can then fill. The user can place headings and data areas wherever he likes on the screen. The user positions fields by means of cursor control keys. The more sophisticated systems will make full use of the display unit's capabilities such as multiple colours, highlighting, divided screens and flashing fields.

The development of multi-user microcomputer systems has brought about the development of multi-user database systems for microcomputers. There is a wide range of database management systems available for microcomputer users to choose from. They do not all have the same in-built features or the same limitations. There are a variety of relational and network database management systems available for the various microcomputer systems. Some database management systems have their own in-built query languages, whereas others are accessed using established programming languages. The microcomputer user must consider the available alternatives carefully before choosing a particular database system.

Distributed databases

The fundamental concept of a database is to hold all the data in a central reservoir. A distributed database is one which conforms logically to the concept of a single administrative collection of data but which is physically distributed among a number of separate computers connected by a network. A computer network may have a number of separate databases which are not related and consequently do not constitute a distributed database. A distributed database exists when related data items are stored on different computers.

A distributed database may be partitioned or replicated, or use a combination of both techniques. A partitioned database holds only one copy of each item of data, the items being stored at the nodes of the network where they will be most frequently required. A replicated database holds multiple copies of the data items, duplicating the data at each of the nodes.

When an attempt is made to access a data item in a partitioned database, the item must first be located. This can be achieved by making use of a single global schema. This schema must be replicated in each of the computers, which can cause problems if the computers are dissimilar. An alternative approach is to maintain a catalogue within each computer of the location of each remote file. If the database is replicated in each computer then the problem is not locating items of data but ensuring that all copies of the database are kept up to date.

Any form of failure in a distributed database necessitates a more complex recovery procedure than for a centralized database. When a failure has been identified, then the state of the database at each of the computers must be established. It may not be easy to determine the cause of a failure quickly because of the physical separation of the various portions of the database. When a failure occurs in one computer the others must be capable of continuing processing. All transactions must be logged so that a complete recovery can be ensured. All the databases must be re-established to an equivalent point in time. This can be achieved by recovering from the logged transactions or by transmitting up-to-date copies of a replicated database.

If the computers are dissimilar then there may be compatibility problems at all levels, from the representation of the data (e.g. character codes and floating-point formats) to the database management system available. Programs written for one machine may not run on another; even the source code versions may not be portable. The greater the differences, the greater the task of accessing information from a remote portion of the database.

Exercises

6.1 What are the advantages of using a database instead of conventional file processing?

6.2 What are the principal stages in creating a database?

6.3 What physical file organizations are suitable for database files?

6.4 What is the purpose of a data dictionary?

6.5 What problems may be caused by two users attempting to access the same database record simultaneously?

6.6 STAFF FILE

EMPLOYEE NUMBER	NAME	SEX	DEPARTMENT	JOB TITLE
03141	SMITH	M	BUS STUDIES	HEAD
02161	JONES	F	MATHEMATICS	LECTURER
01365	WILSON	F	SCIENCE	SECRETARY
01415	BROWN	M	SCIENCE	TECHNICIAN
01837	GREEN	M	MATHEMATICS	LECTURER
01113	BLACK	F	MATHEMATICS	SECRETARY
01145	WHITE	F	SCIENCE	HEAD
01124	JOHNSON	M	SCIENCE	LECTURER
11234	JACKSON	M	SCIENCE	LECTURER
02248	HOWARD	M	BUS STUDIES	LECTURER
21658	DAVIES	F	BUS STUDIES	LECTURER
01728	CAMPBELL	F	MATHEMATICS	HEAD
12634	GORDON	F	BUS STUDIES	SECRETARY
11238	CARTER	F	MATHEMATICS	TECHNICIAN
11347	TAYLOR	M	BUS STUDIES	LECTURER

Represent the serial file as

(a) A sequential file of employee numbers and names with inverted files to show the department, job title and sex of each employee

(b) A linked list file to show the structure of the departments.

7 Database approaches

The different database approaches are distinguished by the conceptual level representation of the data structures. This view of the data structure dictates many of the internal characteristics of the database, such as the way in which the information is represented; it also dictates the operations that may be performed upon the data structures. The three most common approaches are:

The relational (tabular) approach — RAPPORT d.s.
The hierarchical (tree) approach (IMS)
The network (plex) approach. CODASYL model.

The choice of which database management system to use will depend upon the nature of the data to be represented and upon the software available for a particular computer system.

The relational approach is the most recent of the three. Many of the database management systems currently available are based on this approach. The relational approach has been developed from proposals by E. F. Codd of IBM for a generalized relational database system. This chapter looks in particular at the RAPPORT database system. Early databases were based upon the hierarchical approach, which is still favoured by some people for very large databases. The best known of these is IBM's Information Management System (IMS). The network approach considered in this book is the CODASYL model, which is a proposed specification for a database system standard. Many databases based upon the CODASYL model are already implemented.

The relational approach

The important distinction between the various database approaches is the method used to represent the relationships between items of data. The method used by relational databases is to represent the information in tables.

The tables are not dissimilar to a conventional file in which the rows correspond to the records and the columns correspond to the fields. Each row is an instance of the relation and is referred to as a *tuple*. In a relational database the tables are referred to as *relations*. The columns or fields are referred to as the *attributes*, and the complete set of possible values for an attribute is known as the *domain* of that attribute.

It must be possible to uniquely identify each tuple. To achieve this at least one of the attributes must be designated as a *key field*. If the tuple is to be identified by a single key field then the values of the key field must be unique. If more than one key field is used to identify the tuple then the combination of field values must be unique, although the values of individual fields need not necessarily be unique. The unique tuple identifier is termed the *primary key*. The order in which the tuples occur is not significant. The tuples are not ordered within the table.

In certain respects the analogy between tuples and records and between relations and files falls down. For example, a file may contain several different types of record but a relation may contain only one type of tuple. The number of attributes for each tuple remains fixed; there is no equivalent to a record with a variable number of fields. It is not permissible to have repeated groups of attributes, and no attribute within a tuple may have more than one value. A table which meets these requirements is said to be normalized in *first normal form*.

Note In the figures that follow, the symbol # indicates a key field.

Figure 43(a) shows a train timetable as it might be published. It contains repeated groups of train numbers and train times, and fields are left blank where the value can be assumed to be the same as that printed above. This same database is shown normalized into first normal form in Figure 43(b).

This first stage of normalization is achieved by creating a single table with one tuple for every train. The unique key used to identify each tuple is the train number. The table contains a

(a)

DEPARTURE STATION	COUNTRY OF DEPARTURE	CURRENCY OF COUNTRY OF DEPARTURE	DESTINATION STATION	COUNTRY OF DESTINATION	CURRENCY OF COUNTRY OF DESTINATION	TRAIN NO	DEPART	ARRIVE	FARE (STERLING)
LONDON — VICTORIA	ENGLAND	STERLING	PARIS — NORD	FRANCE	FRANCS	1108 404 490	0800 1030 2058	1615 1820 0843	31.00
		STERLING	PARIS — LAZARE	FRANCE	FRANCS	308 3122 1100	0750 1110 2010	1807 2109 0625	31.00
PARIS — NORD	FRANCE	FRANCS	AMSTERDAM CS	HOLLAND	GUILDER	81 283	0719 1023	1230 1632	28.00
		FRANCS	MILAN	ITALY	LIRA	227 23 2525	0741 1230 2252	1700 2100 1055	74.00

(b)

DEPARTURE STATION	COUNTRY OF DEPARTURE	CURRENCY OF COUNTRY OF DEPARTURE	DESTINATION STATION	COUNTRY OF DESTINATION	CURRENCY OF COUNTRY OF DESTINATION	TRAIN # NO	DEPART	ARRIVE	FARE (STERLING)
LONDON — VICTORIA	ENGLAND	STERLING	PARIS — NORD	FRANCE	FRANCS	1108	0800	1615	31.00
LONDON — VICTORIA	ENGLAND	STERLING	PARIS — NORD	FRANCE	FRANCS	404	1030	1820	31.00
LONDON — VICTORIA	ENGLAND	STERLING	PARIS — NORD	FRANCE	FRANCS	490	2058	0843	31.00
LONDON — VICTORIA	ENGLAND	STERLING	PARIS — LAZARE	FRANCE	FRANCS	380	0750	1807	31.00
LONDON — VICTORIA	ENGLAND	STERLING	PARIS — LAZARE	FRANCE	FRANCS	3122	1110	2109	31.00
LONDON — VICTORIA	ENGLAND	STERLING	PARIS — LAZARE	FRANCE	FRANCS	1100	2010	0625	31.00
PARIS — NORD	FRANCE	FRANCS	AMSTERDAM CS	HOLLAND	GUILDER	81	0719	1230	28.00
PARIS — NORD	FRANCE	FRANCS	AMSTERDAM CS	HOLLAND	GUILDER	283	1023	1632	28.00
PARIS — NORD	FRANCE	FRANCS	MILAN	ITALY	LIRA	227	0741	1700	74.00
PARIS — NORD	FRANCE		MILAN		LIRA	23	1230	2100	
PARIS — NORD	FRANCE	FRANCS	MILAN	ITALY	LIRA	2525	2252	1055	74.00

refers to key fields

Figure 43   (a) *TRAINS database before normalization into first normal form*
(b) *TRAINS database after normalization into first normal form*

considerable amount of repeated information. The necessity to store multiple copies of the data can be reduced by redesigning the database as two tables, as shown in Figure 44.

Figure 44(a) contains the repeated groups of information from Figure 43(a) which record the times of each train. Figure 44(b) contains information about each journey, such as the fare, which will not vary with the times of the trains. The cost of a journey between London and Paris remains the same regardless of the time of the train.

The primary key for Figure 44(a) will be the train number, but in Figure 44(b) the primary key is a combination of the departure station and the destination station. Designing the database as two tables in this way reduces the possibility of the database becoming inconsistent. The other attributes describe one or both of these two fields.

If a table is normalized into *second normal form*,

(a)

DEPARTURE STATION	DESTINATION STATION	TRAIN # NO	DEPART	ARRIVE
LONDON — VICTORIA	PARIS — NORD	1108	0800	1615
LONDON — VICTORIA	PARIS — NORD	404	1030	1820
LONDON– VICTORIA	PARIS– NORD	490	2058	0843
LONDON — VICTORIA	PARIS — LAZARE	308	0750	1807
LONDON — VICTORIA	PARIS — LAZARE	3122	1110	2109
LONDON — VICTORIA	PARIS — LAZARE	1100	2010	0625
PARIS — NORD	AMSTERDAM CS	81	0719	1230
PARIS — NORD	AMSTERDAM CS	283	1023	1632
PARIS — NORD	MILAN	227	0741	1700
PARIS — NORD	MILAN	23	1230	2100
PARIS — NORD	MILAN	2525	2252	1055

Figure 44   *(a) TRAINTIMES database*

all of the non-key attributes must describe the primary key. Therefore, to normalize Figure 44(b) into second normal form it must be converted into two tables as shown in Figure 45. The fare is the only attribute which describes both the key fields; the country and currency fields describe only one of the key fields.

A table that is normalized into *third normal form* must satisfy the additional condition that the attributes which describe the primary key must not be dependent upon each other. In Figure 45(a) the primary key is the station; both of the other attributes describe this key field. The other two attributes are, however, dependent upon each other. Figure 46 shows how two third normal form tables can be extracted from the table in Figure 45(a).

The division of one table into two in this manner is called a *projection*. A projection is the selection of one or more columns from one table to create a new table. If two identical tuples are created by this projection then one is removed, as duplicate tuples are not allowed.

The converse of a projection is a *join*, whereby a single table is created from two tables with common attributes.

Integrity rules

Strictly speaking, a relation conforms to the mathematical concepts of a set. Its tuples are elements of the set, which is why the order of the tuples does not matter, and every tuple must be identifiable by a unique primary key. The value of a primary key must not be null. All tuples must be uniquely identifiable but, if the primary key wholly or partially consists of null values, then it cannot be considered as having a unique identifier. A null value is used to indicate that the field value is not known. A primary key field with a null value is contradictory; it implies that a tuple exists with a unique identifier which has no known value. The first rule of integrity, the *entity rule*, is that no primary key value can be null.

By referring to Figure 46(a) it can be seen that the primary key field is the station name, the country is an attribute of this relation. The country is itself a primary key field of a second relationship, the country–currency relation of Figure 46(b). Every different value of the country

(b)

DEPARTURE # STATION	COUNTRY OF DEPARTURE	DESTINATION STATION	COUNTRY OF # DESTINATION	FARE	CURRENCY OF COUNTRY OF DEPARTURE	CURRENCY OF COUNTRY OF DESTINATION
LONDON — VICTORIA	ENGLAND	PARIS — NORD	FRANCE	31.00	STERLING	FRANCS
LONDON — VICTORIA	ENGLAND	PARIS — LAZARE	FRANCE	31.00	STERLING	FRANCS
PARIS — NORD	FRANCE	AMSTERDAM CS	HOLLAND	28.00	FRANCS	GUILDER
PARIS — NORD	FRANCE	MILAN	ITALY	74.00	FRANCS	LIRA

(b) ROUTES database before normalization into second normal form

(a)

STATION #	COUNTRY	CURRENCY
PARIS — NORD	FRANCE	FRANCS
AMSTERDAM CS	HOLLAND	GUILDER
LONDON — VICTORIA	ENGLAND	STERLING
MILAN	ITALY	LIRA
PARIS — LAZARE	FRANCE	FRANCS

(b)

DEPARTURE # STATION	DESTINATION # STATION	FARE (STERLING)
LONDON — VICTORIA	PARIS — NORD	31.00
LONDON — VICTORIA	PARIS — LAZARE	31.00
PARIS — NORD	AMSTERDAM CS	28.00
PARIS — NORD	MILAN	74.00

Figure 45   (a) *RAILWAY-STATION database*
(b) *TRAINFARE database*

(a)

STATION #	COUNTRY
PARIS — NORD	FRANCE
PARIS — LAZARE	FRANCE
LONDON — VICTORIA	ENGLAND
MILAN	ITALY
AMSTERDAM	HOLLAND

(b)

COUNTRY #	CURRENCY
FRANCE	FRANCS
ENGLAND	STERLING
ITALY	LIRA
HOLLAND	GUILDER

Figure 46   (a) *STATION-COUNTRY database*
(b) *MONIES database*

attribute that occurs in Figure 46(a) must have a corresponding tuple in Figure 46(b). This is the second rule of integrity, the *referential rule*. If an attribute of one relation is in turn the single primary key field of a second relation, then every occurrence of the attribute in the first relation must exist as the identifier of a tuple in the second relation.

Relational algebra

One of the characteristics of a relational database is the use of relational algebra. Relational algebra defines a set of relational operators that are applied to relations. The result of a relational operation is always a new relation. Relational operations construct new relations, or tables, from existing relations. Relational operators apply to the complete relation, not just to an individual field or tuple. The basic operations of relational algebra are PROJECT, JOIN and SELECT. However, other operations apart from the basic

relational algebraic operators apply to whole tables. The PROJECT operator constructs a new table by making a copy of the columns of an existing table. In the TRAINTIMES database example the MONIES table (Figure 46(b)) could be created from the relation RAILWAY-STATION (Figure 45(a)) by means of the PROJECT statement:

> PROJECT RAILWAY-STATION WITH
>   (COUNTRY#, CURRENCY)
>   GIVING MONIES

The result is a new table MONIES (Figure 46(b)). If two identical tuples are created by this projection then one is removed, as duplicate tuples are not allowed.

The SELECT operator constructs a new table by selectively extracting tuples from another table. We can create a new table showing the times of trains from LONDON-VICTORIA to PARIS-NORD by means of the SELECT statement:

```
SELECT TRAINTIMES
        WHERE  (DEPARTURE-
STATION = "LONDON-VICTORIA")
        AND   (DESTINATION-
STATION = "PARIS-NORD")
        GIVING  LONDON-TO-PARIS
```

The result is a new table LONDON-TO-PARIS:

DEPARTURE STATION	DESTINATION STATION	TRAIN NO #	DEPART	ARRIVE
LONDON - VICTORIA	PARIS - NORD	1108	0800	1615
LONDON - VICTORIA	PARIS - NORD	404	1030	1820
LONDON - VICTORIA	PARIS - NORD	490	2058	0843

The departure and destination stations are unnecessary now, and the PROJECT operator could be used to create a new table without these attributes:

```
PROJECT LONDON-TO-PARIS WITH
(TRAIN-NO #, DEPART, ARRIVE)
GIVING JOURNEY-TIMES
```

The JOIN operator is used to construct a new table from two existing tables. The two tables must both have an attribute which is defined over the same domain. The new table will have all the attributes of the existing two tables. Each tuple in the new table will have existed in both of the previous tables, with the same attribute value in the field used to join the tables.

If a tuple exists in one of the original tables for which there does not exist a corresponding tuple in the other tables, then a tuple will not be created for the new table.

Consider the following example

```
JOIN TRAINS AND DRIVER BY
    TRAIN-NO# GIVING ROSTA
```

The result is to concatenate the attributes of the TRAINTIMES table (Figure 44(a)) with the DRIVER table (Figure 47(a)) to give a new table, shown in Figure 47(b). The tuples in the TRAINTIMES table which did not have a corresponding tuple in the DRIVER table do not appear in the resulting table.

NB   The syntax of the PROJECT, SELECT and JOIN operations above are not taken from any actual data manipulation language. It should be noted that not all of the languages permit you to name the resulting table. RAPPORT, used elsewhere in this book, does not include basic relational operators that apply to whole tables, and consequently is not considered by some to be a true relational database.

Defining a relational database
Once the relations have been normalized, the database can be defined. This is achieved by specifying the relations in terms of the database definition language. The input file defining the

(a)

TRAIN NO #	DATE	DRIVER
1108	11/3	M. JONES
404	10/3	R. SMITH
490	12/3	B. DAVIES
227	11/3	A. JAQUES
23	11/3	K. MONESPIERRE
2525	12/3	D. MEYET
1636	10/3	A. JACKSON

Figure 47   *(a) DRIVER*

(b)

TRAIN # NO	DEPARTURE STATION	DESTINATION STATION	DEPART	ARRIVE	DATE	DRIVER
1108	LONDON — VICTORIA	PARIS — NORD	0800	1615	11/3	M. JONES
404	LONDON — VICTORIA	PARIS — NORD	1030	1820	10/3	R. SMITH
490	LONDON — VICTORIA	PARIS — NORD	2058	0843	12/3	B. DAVIES
227	PARIS — NORD	MILAN	0741	1700	11/3	A. JACQUES
23	PARIS — NORD	MILAN	1230	2100	11/3	K. MONESPIERRE
2525	PARIS — NORD	MILAN	2252	1052	12/3	D. MEYET

(b) ROSTA

database (database definition file) will then be processed to create an empty database. The processing of the database definition file is equivalent to the compilation of a program – only in this case the program is written in the data definition language. The language has no executable instructions; it simply reserves areas of store.

Each table must be defined separately; each field or attribute of the table must be specified, giving the size and type of each field.

Example to define the TRAINTIMES database of Figure 44(a)

System R database definition
```
CREATE TABLE TRAINTIMES
    (DEPARTURE # CHAR (20) NONULL),
    DESTINATION # (CHAR (20)),
    TRAIN-NO INTEGER
    DEPART INTEGER
    ARRIVE INTEGER
```

RAPPORT database definition
```
    FILE TRAINTIMES
    SLOTS 500
    FIELDS
    DEPARTURE (5) CHARS PKEY
    DESTINATION (5) CHARS PKEY
    TRAIN-NO
    DEPART
    ARRIVE
```

The syntax used by the two systems differs, but the semantics are essentially the same. Both examples define the relation TRAINTIMES from Figure 44(a). This relation has two key fields (indicated by # in System R and by PKEY in RAPPORT). The sizes of character fields are specified differently, in that the number of characters making up the field is specified in System R and the number of words is specified in RAPPORT. RAPPORT fields are integer fields by default. System R permits the declaration of INTEGER fields, occupying a whole word, and SMALLINT fields, which occupy a half word. RAPPORT permits fields to be declared in BITS to provide small binary fields.

Addressing techniques
The internal representation of a relation must enable each tuple to be identified by its key fields. Several addressing techniques for identifying and retrieving tuples are currently used. Rapport utilizes the following three methods:

1 A hashing function based upon the primary key (PKEY) field value is used to store each tuple. Any search based upon the primary key fields will use the hashing function to locate the tuple.
2 A secondary index may be specified for frequently accessed fields which do not form part of the primary key. The indexed fields must be defined when the database is created. Indexes take up extra storage space but provide faster access to secondary fields.
3 A linear search must be performed to locate tuples using a secondary field which has no index. If a high proportion of the tuples in the relation are required then this can be a suitable method.

Accessing the relational database: RAPPORT query language
A relational database may be accessed by including data manipulation language statements within an application program, or by interrogating the database from a terminal using a query language. The RAPPORT commands to access a RAPPORT database are described below. RAPPORT terminology refers to files and records rather than relations and tuples.

The RAPPORT interactive query language (IQL) enables the user to interrogate a RAPPORT database from a terminal. The user may type in any of the IQL commands, but none will be performed until the user specifically instructs the computer to do so. The IQL commands enable the user to

Search the database for particular occurrences of relations
Update the contents of the database
Perform arithmetic calculations
Format output reports

The user's view of the database is provided

through buffers. The buffers are the user's interface with the database. There is one buffer for each different record type. When a record is fetched from the database its values will be placed in the buffer. Similarly the user may build up a new record in the buffer before writing it to the database.

Commands to retrieve records from the database
The FETCH command retrieves a single record that satisfies the conditions specified. The conditions are expressed as Boolean relationships connected by logical operators.

For example, the TRAINFARE database defined above can be used to find the cost of a train journey from LONDON to PARIS by the command:

> FETCH TRAINFARE WHERE (DEPAR-
> TURE = 'LONDON-VICTORIA') AND
> DESTINATION = 'PARIS-LAZARE')

If more than one record exists that satisfies the condition, then the first one encountered by the DBMS will be returned.

The SEARCH command is used to retrieve all records that satisfy the condition specified. If no conditions are specified then all the records will be returned. The records are returned one at a time in the order in which they are encountered by the hashing algorithm. If the records are required in a particular sequence, then this may be specified by the ORDER command. For example,

> ORDER TRAINTIMES DEPART UP
>   SEARCH TRAINTIMES WHERE (DE-
> PARTURE = 'LONDON-VICTORIA') AND
> (DESTINATION = 'PARIS-NORD')

The sequence above will give the times of trains from LONDON-VICTORIA to PARIS-NORD in chronological order.

The FETCH and SEARCH commands place the records retrieved into a buffer. The contents of the buffer can be displayed on the terminal by a SHOW or WRITE command. The SHOW command displays the current values of all the fields in a record. The WRITE command permits the user to specify which fields are to be displayed; the fields may be taken from several different records.

Updating the database
The user may alter the contents of the buffer fields by the SET command. For example, to alter the time of a train:

> SET TRAINTIMES. DEPART = 1358
> SET TRAINTIMES. ARRIVE = 2228

The SET command can be used to create a new record or to update the field values of an existing record. An updated record can be written to the database by using either the STORE or UPDATE commands. The STORE command will place a record in the database regardless of whether a record already exists with the same primary key values. The UPDATE command can also be used to place a record in the database, but the record will only be written if no other record with the same primary key values exists.

A new record can be written to the database by means of the INSERT command. Records can be deleted by means of the DELETE command; all records that satisfy the condition specified will be removed.

Performing arithmetic calculations
RAPPORT permits a user to compute a value for a data item by means of the SET command. For example, to increase a train fare by 5%:

> SET TRAINFARE.FARE =
>   TRAINFARE.FARE * 1.05

An expression on the right-hand side of a SET command may include any of the operators *, /, +, −, and brackets may be used to indicate the order of precedence.

SUM, COUNT and AVG are arithmetic commands which apply to all occurrences of the record which satisfy the conditions specified. For example,

> COUNT TRAINTIMES WHERE (DEPAR-
> TURE = 'PARIS-NORD') AND
> (DESTINATION = 'AMSTERDAM-CS')

will calculate how many trains travel from PARIS-NORD to AMSTERDAM-CS each day.

The result will be placed in every field of the buffer containing the TRAINTIMES record.

If no conditions are specified then all records will be included. For example,

COUNT ROUTES

will inform the user how many records there are in the ROUTES database.

SUM will accumulate the values of all numeric fields in the records that satisfy the condition. Similarly, AVG will calculate the average value of all the numeric fields in the records that satisfy the conditions.

MAX and MIN calculate the maximum and minimum field values for each numeric field.

Formatting output reports
The output from a RAPPORT query session can be directed to the terminal or a file for subsequent printing. The user can specify the layout of the output and the format of all field values. He can specify the position of the data items and, if the output is to be produced in paged format, the headings and footings to appear on each page.

The format statement can be used to specify the layout of individual fields or fields of a particular type. For example:

1 An individual numeric item which is to be printed with three digits before the decimal point and two following:

FORMAT TRAINFARE.FARE : 3,2

2 All character fields are to be printed with sixteen character positions following three spaces:

FORMAT CHARACTER : 3,16

The position of the data items on the screen or page is achieved by a combination of the WRITE and FORMAT commands. The WRITE command indicates the column in which printing is to start. The HOLD WRITE command indicates that the next WRITE command is to be printed on the same line. For example, outputting the departure and destination station and train fare upon the same line:

HOLD WRITE 5 TRAINFARE.

DEPARTURE, DESTINATION
WRITE 50 TRAINFARE.FARE

None of the above commands will be obeyed until an EXECUTE (EX) command is typed in. When EX is input all commands input since the previous EXECUTE command will then be obeyed.

All commands which change the contents of the database are carried out in a transaction. The start of a transaction is indicated by the TRANSACT command and the end of a transaction by a COMMIT command. For example, to increase all train fares by 5%:

```
TRANSACT
    SEARCH TRAINFARE
        SET TRAINFARE.FARE =
        TRAINFARE.FARE * 1.05
        UPDATE TRAINFARE
    LOOP
COMMIT
EX
```

No changes are made to the content of the database until the COMMIT command is obeyed. It is up to the user to decide whether all the updates constitute a single transaction, as in the example above, or whether each update should be a separate transaction. This decision will determine the extent of recovery necessary should any error occur during the transaction. If the user wishes to undo all updates performed since the last COMMIT command, then this can be achieved by a BACKOUT command. A BACKOUT command rolls the system back to the state it was in when the previous COMMIT command was obeyed.

The sequence of commands input prior to an EXECUTE command can include conditional and iterative statements, which enable the user to structure the commands.

The IF statement has the format

```
IF condition-1
    THEN command-block-1
    [ELSIF condition-2
        THEN command-block-2]
    [ELSE command-block-3]
ENDIF
```

and the WHILE statement has the format

> WHILE condition
> > DO command-block
> ENDWHILE

NB   The contents of the square brackets are optional.

Command sequences
If a sequence of commands is to be performed more than once, then they can be stored as a command sequence. This command sequence must be compiled by the IQL PREPARE command before it can be run. The command sequence can be invoked by the RUN command. IQL has its own editor for creating and altering command sequences.

RAPPORT program commands
RAPPORT program commands were initially developed for incorporation in FORTRAN prog-

rams, but COBOL and Pascal interfaces are now also available. The commands to access and update database records are essentially the same as for the query language. The commands each have an extra parameter which is a reply word used to indicate whether any error has occurred during the execution of the command. This reply word should be examined after each RAPPORT command has been obeyed. There are no RAPPORT program commands to produce statistics or reports, as these facilities can be provided by the host programming language.

All database files that are to be accessed from within the host program must be declared at the beginning of the program. The format of the records declared within the program can be a subset of the physical records. All commands to access the database must be formed by START-RAPPORT and ENDRAPPORT commands; these commands correspond to the OPEN and CLOSE statements used with conventional files.

The hierarchical approach

Hierarchical database systems are based upon hierarchical tree structures. The best known and by far the most commonly used hierarchical

database system is IBM's Information Management System (IMS). IMS was originally developed as a joint venture between IBM and the

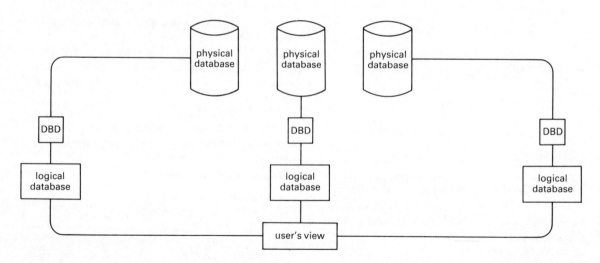

Figure 48   *IMS database structure*

Rockwell International Corporation. The first version was introduced in 1969.

The IMS database (see Figure 48) is based upon the concept of several physical databases each separately defined by its own database definition (DBD). The DBD defines a single tree structure, and the corresponding physical database contains each occurrence of this tree. The definition of the tree structure is known as the database definition record.

The user's view of the database is of a collection of logical databases, where a logical database is a subset of the corresponding physical database.

Both the physical and logical databases are defined using IMS utility programs. The definitions are specified using macro instructions which are converted into object code by the utility programs. The database definition for each physical database is stored in the database definition library. The user's view of the database is specified in a program specification block (PSB). One PSB is required for each application program. The PSB will contain a definition for each of the logical databases to be accessed by the program. The definition of each logical database is contained within a program communication block (PCB). The object code generated for the PSB is held in the PSB library.

The application program itself will contain statements which access the contents of the database. The statements are written as subroutine calls within the host program which may be written in COBOL, PL1 or IBM 370 assembler language.

Each entry in the tree is referred to as a segment. Each different segment has an identifying type number. The root segment is type number 1, and other segments are numbered from left to right and down the tree. Each segment has only one parent segment (except the root segment which has no parent) and may have several children segments of different types. A parent segment may also have several children of the same segment type; these are referred to as twins.

The football league database shown in Figure 49 illustrates the physical database structure of a hierarchical database. The physical database will contain one physical database record for each of the football league clubs. Each club has a single root segment, but the root segment will have several children. The club will have been playing in the league for a number of seasons, resulting in there being several team record segments for the club. The club should also have at least eleven players on their team list, resulting in at least eleven occurrences of the PLAYER-SEG. For

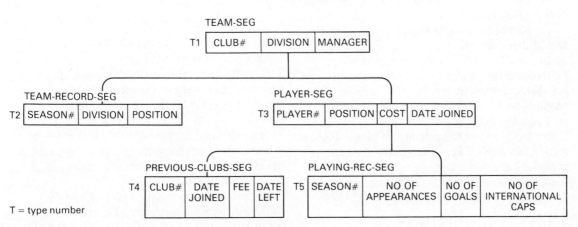

Figure 49 *Physical database record: hierarchical tree structure*

(a)

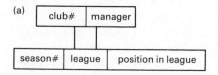

(b)

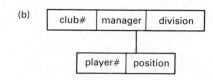

Figure 50   (a) *Logical database record for club's history*
(b) *Logical database record for team list*

each player there is a record of his playing performance each year as well as a history of the clubs he has played for.

The user's view of the database is made up of a collection of logical databases. Each logical database may be a subset of the corresponding physical database. The subset must contain the root segment, and if any dependent segment is omitted all that segment's children must also be omitted from the definition of the logical database record. Two examples of logical database records extracted from the football league database are shown in Figure 50.

As can be seen from the example, the logical database may be constructed by omitting segment types and by omitting fields from a segment type. The segments contained in the user's logical database are referred to as sensitive segments. As will be shown later, the data manipulation language instruction set permits the user to insert, alter or delete an occurrence of a segment. The instructions do not operate upon the logical database but upon the physical database, which means that if a parent segment entry is deleted so also are all of its children.

The identity of a segment entry is given by the key field of the segment and each of its ancestors in the tree. The full identifier is known as the hierarchical key, and is given by the segment type number and segment entry key for each segment on the hierarchical path down the tree, from the root segment to the segment required. For example, in the football league database of Figure 49, the hierarchical key to access the segment containing the playing performance for the Melchester Rovers star player known as Roy of the Rovers, for the 1983/84 season, would be

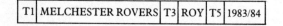

The segment type numbers T1, T3 and T5 identify the branch of the tree being accessed. The keys following the segment type numbers identify the particular segment required. The segment type number is recorded in a prefix that precedes each segment. This prefix also includes a flag which is set if the segment is deleted.

IMS internal storage structure
Each record segment is identified by its unique hierarchical key. The method used to access the segment depends upon the way in which the segments are organized in store. IMS provides four access methods within the hierarchical scheme. These are

HSAM	hierarchical sequential access method
HISAM	hierarchical indexed sequential access method
HDAM	hierarchical direct access method
HIDAM	hierarchical indexed direct access method

Hierarchical sequential access method
(ACCESS = HSAM)
The hierarchical structure of the record is represented entirely by the physical position of the segments. Each segment is followed by its own descendants. The structure is restrictive because although it is possible to retrieve information from the database, it is not possible to update or delete segments without generating a new version of the database.

Records are stored sequentially. The only method of access is a sequential search. Because of the nature of this method, databases organized using HSAM structure may be held on magnetic

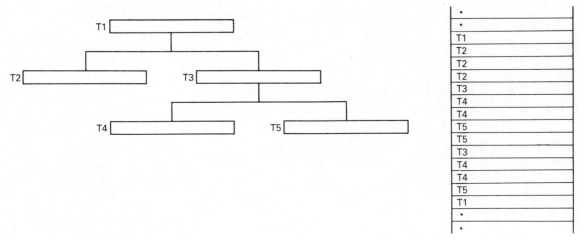

Figure 51   *Hierarchical sequential access*

tape. Figure 51 shows a hierarchical sequential access record structure, and illustrates how each segment follows its parent in store.

Hierarchical indexed sequential access method (ACCESS = HISAM)

In a HISAM structure the segments of each record are stored contiguously in hierarchical key order. Starting with the root segment, each segment is followed by its immediate descendants and then its twins. An index is used to locate the root segment. Other segments are located by a sequential search of the record.

In a conventional memory the index will locate the physical block containing the root segment of a record. If the complete record is too large to be contained within a single physical block then overflow blocks are used. The overflow blocks are linked in a chain. A sequential search of the chained blocks is used to access a particular segment. See Figure 52.

Segments may be inserted and deleted. If a new root segment is to be inserted (which corresponds to inserting a new record into a file) then a new entry is created in the index but the root segment itself is placed directly into an overflow block. If a dependent segment is to be inserted then it must be placed in its correct position in the hierarchical key sequence. The segment that currently occupies this position and all the segments that follow

it must be moved along to make room for the new segment. A segment that is to be deleted is not actually removed from the block but marked by a flag.

In a virtual memory each data page contains a number of records (Figure 53). The segments within a record are held in hierarchical key sequence order, as before. When records are initially allocated to pages, the pages are only part filled to allow for expansion of the file.

A B-tree index is used to locate the root segment of each record. The index contains a pointer to the lowest record key value of each data page. If when a record is inserted there is insufficient room within the data page for the record, then an overflow page is used and chained to the data page.

Hierarchical indexed direct access method (ACCESS = HIDAM)

This structure also uses an index to locate a particular root segment. The appropriate subordinate segment can then be reached by following a chain of pointers. The pointers may be organized in one of two ways.

1   *Hierarchical pointers* (POINTER = HIER/ HIERBWD)   A segment will point to the first of its dependents in hierarchical key sequence order (link (a)) in Figure 54. If a segment has no dependents, it will point to its

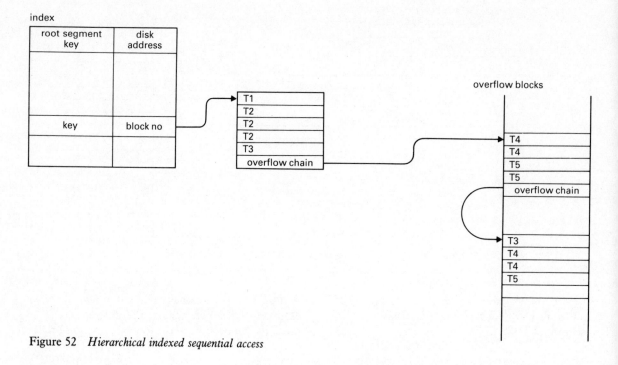

Figure 52   *Hierarchical indexed sequential access*

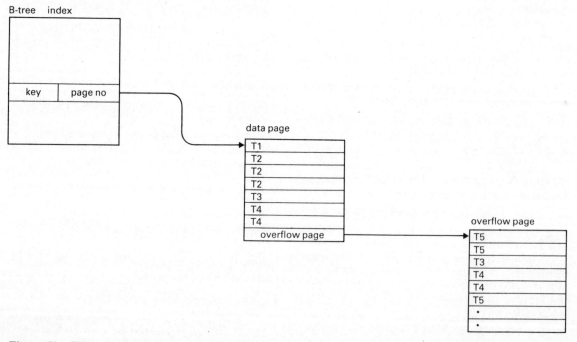

Figure 53   *Hierarchical indexed sequential access in a paged memory*

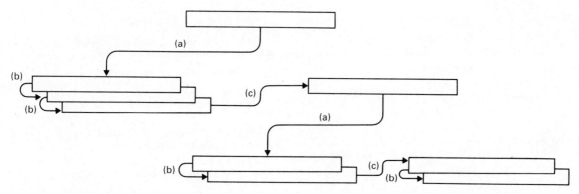

Figure 54 *Hierarchical pointers*

twin (link (b)). If it has no remaining twin then it will point either to the first segment of the next segment type (link (c)) or to its own parent's twin. The pointers may be bidirectional, in which case HIERBWD must be specified.

2 *Child/twin pointers* (POINTER = TWIN/ TWINBWD)   Each occurrence of a segment type has a pointer to the first occurrence of each of its children (link (d)) in Figure 55. Each child segment occurrence will have a pointer to the next occurrence of the same segment type (link (f)). The pointers may be bidirectional (TWINBWD), in which case the pointers between occurrences of the same child segment type will be in both directions. The last occurrence of a child segment type will have a pointer to its parent.

It is possible to combine both types of pointer

within the same physical record. The relationship between each segment and its direct descendants is specified separately for each segment type.

Hierarchical direct access method
(ACCESS = HDAM)

In a HDAM structure the root segments are accessed using a hashing algorithm rather than an index. When a root segment is to be inserted the hashing algorithm generates the address of a storage record in which the segment is to be placed. More than one segment may be placed in the same storage record. The root segments within a storage record are chained together in key sequence order. If the storage record is already full when a new root segment is to be inserted, then it is placed in the nearest storage record with free space available. The illusion that it is in the correct storage record is maintained by

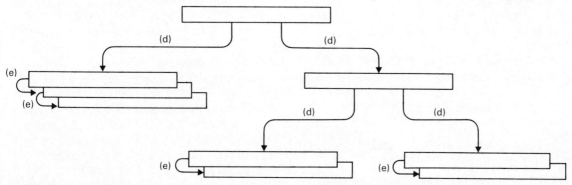

Figure 55 *Child/twin pointers*

Mnemonic	Meaning	Operation
GU	GET UNIQUE	Fetch the first occurrence of the segment that satisfies the qualifying conditions specified
GN	GET NEXT	Get the next occurrence of the segment
GNP	GET NEXT WITHIN PARENT	This function operates in the same way as GET NEXT except that the next segment is only fetched if it has the same parent
GHU	GET HOLD UNIQUE	The DELETE and REPLACE operations must be preceded by a GET HOLD operation
GHN	GET HOLD NEXT	
GHNP	GET HOLD NEXT WITHIN PARENT	
ISRT	INSERT	Insert a new segment as a child to a specified parent
DLET	DELETE	Delete a specified segment
REPL	REPLACE	The segment to be replaced must first be fetched by a GET HOLD operation and then when the data values have been amended the segment can be replaced

Figure 56   *Data manipulation language (DL/I) operations*

placing the root segment in its correct position in the chain.

The subordinate segments are accessed using pointers in the same way as in a HIDAM structure. The segments are placed as close to the root segment as possible in order to speed up retrieval operations.

Data manipulation in a hierarchical database

The data manipulation language (DL/I) instructions are invoked by means of a subroutine call from the host language program. The subroutine has a number of parameters which specify

The operation required (OPER); see Figure 56 for the set of permissible operations.
The program control block which identifies the logical database (PCB-LINK).
The input/output buffer into which the data segment is to be received or in which data values are to be stored in preparation for insertion into the database (IOBUFF).
Qualifying conditions, referred to as 'search segment arguments', which will identify the path to the segment required (ROOT-COND, COND2).

The format of such a call from a COBOL program would be

CALL 'CBLTDL1' USING OPER, PCB-
   LINK, IOBUFF, ROOT-COND, COND2.

An example of a subroutine call to fetch a specific segment from the football league database is

CALL 'CBLTDL1' USING 'GU', PCB-
   AREA, PLAYING-REC-AREA,
      TEAM-SEG (TEAM = 'MELCHESTER
      ROVERS'),
      PLAYER-SEG (PLAYER = 'ROY   '),
   RECORD-SEG

The operation (OPER) may be any of those from Figure 56. These operations permit the programmer to fetch, insert, delete or replace segments. The segments required are specified by the search segment arguments.

If when fetching a segment more than one segment satisfies the conditions, then GET UNIQUE will fetch the first segment encountered that meets these conditions. GET NEXT can be used to fetch each of the other segments which satisfy the same conditions in turn. The order in which the segments are returned depends upon the storage organization specified. When a segment is accessed using a GET instruction of any kind, then the data values will be transferred into the buffer area specified in the call statement. The buffer area is declared in the data declaration section of the host program. In the example above, PLAYING-REC-AREA would be declared in the working-storage section of a COBOL program.

The search segment arguments are used to identify the path to a particular segment. The names of every segment on the path must be specified. It is possible also to associate conditions with the segment names. The conditions are expressed in the form

segment name (conditional expression)

where each conditional expression may be constructed as a combination of conditional expressions joined by the logical operators AND(*) and OR(+). A simple conditional expression has the format

field name   relational operator
comparative value

In the example above the segment names specifying the branch of the tree required are TEAM-SEG, PLAYER-SEG and RECORD-SEG. The first two segment names are qualified by conditions, specifying a particular football club and a particular player. The RECORD-SEG is not qualified, which means that the first segment encountered describing this player's playing record will be returned by the subroutine call.

The field name may refer to any of the fields in the segment, not just key fields. The relational operator may be any of the conventional operators ($<$, $>$, $<=$, $=>$, $\neq$ or $=$). The comparative value must be equal in size and type to the field specified. The comparison is made bit by bit from left to right.

Communication between the program and the database management system is achieved through the program communications block (PCB). The PCB is an area defined in the host program which contains

The name of the physical database being accessed
The level number and name of the segment last accessed (this information is placed in the PCB area by the DBMS)
A status code which is used to indicate the success of the operation just performed.

IMS database operation

The first stage in accessing the database is to initialize the system. This is achieved by an IMS

loading routine called the regional controller. The regional controller ensures that all the modules and definition blocks necessary to run the application program are loaded. These are shown in Figure 57.

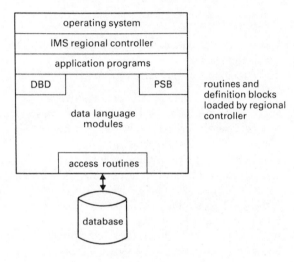

Figure 57 *IMS database access*

When the necessary routines have been loaded, the operating system can load the applications program.

Access to the database is provided through the data language modules, which access the database definition blocks (DBD) and the program specification blocks (PSB) to obtain the necessary information to access the data. The DBD will contain details of the storage method used and the data language module calls the appropriate access method to access the data.

There are difficulties in representing some data structures using only hierarchical tree structures. The restrictions are caused by the limitations that a segment may have only one parent. The timetables data structure illustrated in Figure 36(b) could not be represented in a hierarchical database. It requires a network approach.

The network approach

In April 1971 the Data Base Task Group, which is a subcommittee of CODASYL (Committee on Data Systems Languages), produced a report now known simply as the DBTG report. The report outlined proposals for three languages.

A schema data description language (schema DDL)
A subschema data description language (sub-schema DDL)
A data manipulation language (DML).

These proposals were based upon a network approach to databases. The schema DDL was a new language designed to describe just such a database; the other two proposals were extensions to the COBOL programming language.

Later in 1971 a new committee, the CODASYL Data Description Language Committee, was formed. This committee assumed responsibility for the development of the schema data description language. The schema data description language is intended for use with a variety of programming languages, not just COBOL. The responsibility for the development of the subschema data description language and the data manipulation language for COBOL now belongs to the CODASYL COBOL committee.

Most databases which use the network approach are based upon the DBTG report. Some systems, however, such as Honeywell's Integrated Data Store (IDS), predate the report. IDS had a strong influence upon the subsequent DBTG report.

The schema describes the complete database in terms of data items, data aggregates, records, areas and sets. Records in a network database are analogous to the COBOL record structure. In a COBOL record, both group and elementary fields are permitted. A data aggregate is equivalent to a COBOL group field and a data item is equivalent to a COBOL elementary field.

The subschema describes a subset of the database as viewed from a user's application program. The user's view may consist of a subset of the database's records. The record defined in the user's program may be constructed from a subset of the fields defined in the database schema.

The set concept is one of the most distinctive features of the network approach. The set defines the relationship between record types. Each occurrence of a set consists of one owner record and one or more member records. For each occurrence of the owner record there will be one occurrence of the set.

Any record may be the owner record of one or more sets, and any record may be the member record of one or more sets. A record may be the owner of one set and the member record of another set.

The order of the member records within a set will be dependent upon

1 A sort key, or
2 The position in which the record was placed in the database (see 'Data Definition Language' later in this chapter).

If a record is a member of more than one set, then the order of the records may be different in each of the sets.

The realm concept is another important feature of the network approach. A realm is a logical subset of the database, analogous to a file in a non-database application. A realm consists of a collection of records. There is no defined order to the records. The records can be of several different record types and a record type can be defined in more than one realm. A number of realms can be defined in the same subschema.

Two diagrammatic notations are used to describe a set: 'pointer chain' diagrams and Bachman's 'data structure' diagrams (Figure 58). Pointer chain diagrams are useful to illustrate the pointers that can be used to reference records from within a set. The data structure diagrams are more useful when it comes to illustrating the data structures that may be constructed using sets.

Pointers

Within the schema it is possible to specify the type of pointers which are to be used to chain the

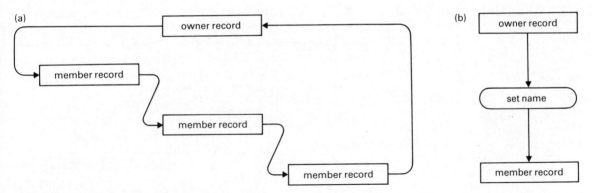

Figure 58   *(a) Example of a pointer chain diagram*
(b) Example of a data structure diagram

records together. The type of pointers specified will depend upon the nature of the processing required. The set mode defines the type of pointers required. The basic options are to specify that the member records are to be chained or linked by a *pointer array*.

A chain provides serial access to all occurrences of the member records. Each of the member records points to the next in turn. The last member record points back to the owner record (Figure 59).

If processing is required in the opposite direction then this may be achieved by specifying LINKED TO PRIOR in the set mode clause. This will establish a series of backward links, enabling the records to be processed in the reverse direction. In Figure 60 the backward links are shown by dotted lines.

All member records of a set may be linked to the owner record. This is specified within the definition of the set by LINKED TO OWNER. In Figure 61 the owner links are shown by dotted lines.

A record can have both backward and owner pointers as well as the forward links. For each set having a record which is either a member or owner with chain pointers, extra storage space is required within the record. This can amount to a considerable storage requirement. A single set accessed via a pointer chain can be held as a single linked list, a two-way linked list or a cyclic linked list.

If a set is declared as using pointer arrays then the owner record contains a list of all member records, represented by a link to each member record (Figure 62). The member records may contain pointers back to the owner.

The relationship between member records is preserved by the order of the links within the owner record.

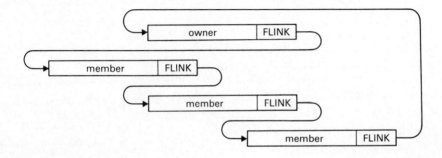

Figure 59   *Forward pointers*

FLINK .... forward link

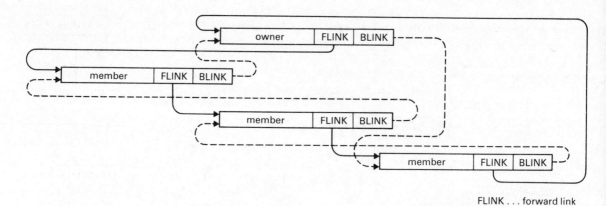

FLINK . . . forward link
BLINK . . . backward link

Figure 60   *Backward pointers (LINKED TO PRIOR)*

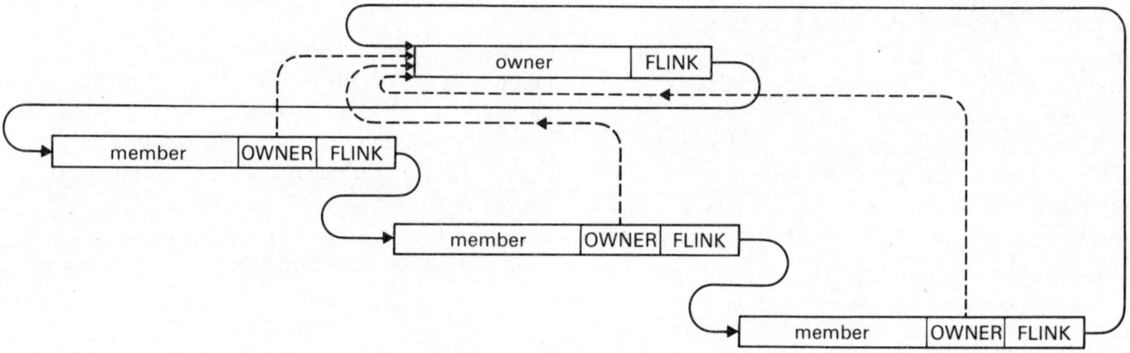

Figure 61   *Owner pointers (LINKED TO OWNER)*

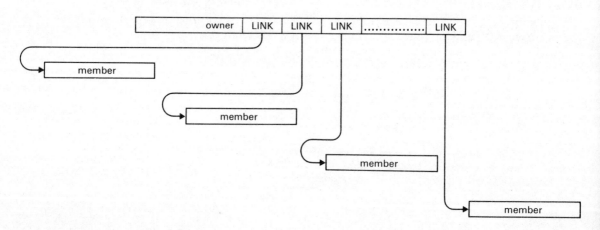

Figure 62   *Pointer arrays*

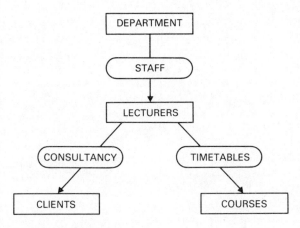

Figure 63 *A tree structure*

Processing of the records using pointers is restricted to serial access. If the member records are chained each record has to be retrieved from the database in order to find the links to the next record.

The order of the member records within a set can be specified as being

1 Sorted in either ascending or descending order on a user-specified sort key.
2 Positioned as the FIRST record (starting from the owner record), the LAST record or immediately PRIOR to or NEXT to the current record.
3 Immaterial.

Data structures

The set concept permits complex data structures to be represented. A hierarchical tree structure can be constructed by declaring the owner record of one set as the member of the set above (Figure 63). The tree can be traversed by following the pointers.

In a hierarchical database a child is restricted to a single parent. The structure illustrated in Figure 63 assumes that each course has only one lecturer, whereas in fact a course is quite likely to have several lecturers. To represent this we need a network structure. In a database based upon the network approach it is possible for a child to have more than one parent, i.e. a record may be a member of more than one set (Figure 64).

It is possible for cyclic structures to be constructed in which a child can also be one of its own ancestors (Figure 65).

Data definition language

The database adminstrator defines the schema using the data definition language. The schema description contains a definition of every record in the database and the set of relationships between records. The record description is equivalent to a COBOL record description. For example, a description of a lecturer record within a time-tabling database:

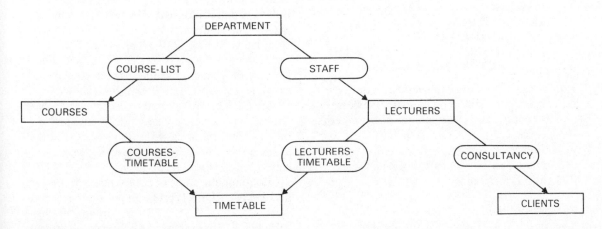

Figure 64 *A network structure*

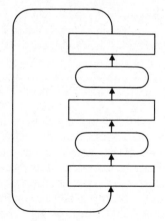

Figure 65   *A cyclic network*

RECORD NAME IS LECTURERS
        DUPLICATES ARE NOT
        ALLOWED FOR LEC-NAME.
02   LEC-NAME PIC X(30).
02   LEC-GRADE PIC X(4).
02   SALARY PIC 9(5)V99.

Clauses may be included in the record definitions to indicate to the database management system the basis for locating a record occurrence, the actions that may be performed on the whole record or upon individual fields, and permissible values for particular fields.

The set description specifies the relationship between records. For example:

SET NAME IS STAFF
    OWNER IS DEPARTMENT
    MEMBER IS LECTURER
        LINKED TO OWNER
        INSERTION IS AUTOMATIC
        RETENTION IS OPTIONAL

Additional clauses allow the database administrator to specify the logical relationship between members of the same sets, and to specify whether the members of a set are sorted and if so the sort keys. Indexes to speed up access to member records can be set up by means of a SET SELECTION clause.

Subschema definition
The subschema is defined by means of a subschema data definition language (DDL). A

```
TITLE DIVISION.
SS COURSES WITHIN TIMETABLES.
MAPPING DIVISION.
ALIAS SECTION.
AD RECORD TEACHERS IS LECTURERS.
AD RECORD CLASSES IS COURSES.
AD SET TEACHERS-TIMETABLE IS LECTURERS-TIMETABLE.
ADD SET CLASS-TIMETABLE IS COURSES-TIMETABLE.
AD TEACHER IS LEC-NAME.
AD TEACHER-GRADE IS LEC-GRADE.
AD CLASS IS COURSES-TITLE.
AD FORM-TEACHER IS COURSE-TUTOR.

STRUCTURE DIVISION.
REALM SECTION.
RD DEPT-REALM CONTAINS DEPARTMENT, COURSES,
TEACHERS, TIMETABLE RECORDS.

SET SECTION.
SD STAFF.
SD CLASS-TIMETABLE
   SET SELECTION IS CLASS IN CLASSES.
SD TEACHERS-TIMETABLE.

RECORD SECTION.
01  TEACHERS.
    02   LEC-NAME PIC X(30).
    02   LEC-GRADE PIC X(4).
    02   SALARY PIC 9(5)V99.

01  DEPARTMENT.
    02   DEPT-NAME PIC X(20).
    02   DEPT-GRADE PIC 99.

01  CLASSES.
    02   CLASS PIC X(30).
    02   FORM-TEACHER PIC X(30).

01  TIMETABLE.
    02   DAY    PIC 9.
    02   PERIOD    PIC 99.
    02   SUBJECT    PIC X(20).
    02   ROOM    PIC X(4).
```

Figure 66   *Sample subschema definition*

subschema defined using the COBOL subschema DDL has three divisions. The title division gives a name to the subschema and identifies the schema to which it refers. The mapping division is used to define alternative names by which database elements may be referred to within the subschema and the COBOL program. The structure division specifies the records sets and features which comprise the subschema. An example of a subschema definition is shown in Figure 66. This sample subschema illustrates how the user's program may take a different view of the database. In this case the database is regarded as a school's timetable database rather than a college's timetable database.

Specifying the name of a subschema in the data division of a COBOL program reserves an area of store for each of the record types defined in the subschema. These areas of store form the 'user's work area'. Any records retrieved from the database will be placed in this area. Conversely records to be stored in the database are built up in this area.

Data manipulation language

The data manipulation language statements can be summarized as

The FIND statement, which locates particular records
Statements to revise the membership of sets
Statements to fetch, update, store and delete the records pointed to by the currency indicators.

The DML statements are incorporated into a COBOL program. The usual COBOL language statements can be applied to the record field values.

Currency indicators and the FIND statement

An important concept in a CODASYL database is that of currency. The database management system maintains a table of currency indicators. A currency indicator is a pointer to the most recently accessed record of each record type, set type, realm or the record most recently accessed by the program (the most recently accessed record of the program is referred to as the 'current record of the run unit').

The FIND statement is used to locate a particular database record. As a result, the currency indicator for the run unit will be modified to point to this record. Other currency indicators appropriate to the record type, set and realm will also be modified unless the user specifies that the previous values for these indicators are to be retained.

The FIND statement can be used in a number of different ways.

1   *To locate a record of a particular record type* by specifying the value of one or more fields. The FIND statement will locate a record of the appropriate type which matches these values:

MOVE 'SMITH' TO LEC-NAME
FIND ANY LECTURER
   USING LEC-NAME IN LECTURER

The FIND statement can be used to locate any further records with duplicate values for the specified fields. For example, it could be used to determine whether there are any more lecturers with the name of SMITH:

FIND DUPLICATE LECTURER
   USING LEC-NAME IN LECTURER

2   *To locate the owner record of a set*   It is important to remember that there are several occurrences of a set. There is one occurrence of the set for every occurrence of the owner record. Each owner record of the set will have one or more member records. The currency indicator for the set will point to the most recently accessed record, which may be either an owner record or a member record. The currency indicator will identify the occurrence of the set. The FIND statement can be used to locate the owner record of the current occurrence of the set. The sequence of statements below will locate a record for a lecturer then, using this as the currency indicator for the set, will locate the department for which the lecturer works.

MOVE 'SMITH' TO LEC-NAME
FIND ANY LECTURER
   USING LEC-NAME IN LECTURER
FIND OWNER WITHIN STAFF-SET

3   *To locate a member record of a set*   The currency indicator for the set points to one record of the set which identifies the occurrence of the set. The FIND statement can be used to locate any particular member record of that set. This may be the first record, the last record, any record that matches specified values, the next record or the previous record.

4   *To locate a record using its database key*   The database key is in fact the record's address within the database and is not usually known by the user. However, when a record is 'found' then the user may assign its address to a 'keep list'. If the record is required again then it may be located using this 'keep list'. The keep list is used when processing the same string of records more than once. The KEEP statement places a database key on the keep list. A keep list can be emptied or an

individual key removed from the keep list by the FREE statement.

Statements to revise the membership of sets
There are three statements affecting set membership. These are the CONNECT, DISCONNECT and RECONNECT statements. An occurrence of a set consists of one owner record and several member records. The statements affect the membership of the records to the set. The CONNECT statement joins a member record to the set; the DISCONNECT statement logically removes a member record from the set; and the RECONNECT statement logically removes a member record from one set and joins it to another.

The application of the statements is dependent upon the specification of the set in the schema. The schema must include a specification of the criteria for inserting and retaining member records for each set. Insertion can be automatic or manual. If insertion is specified as being automatic, then when an occurrence of the member record is created and stored in the database, the database management system will automatically connect it to the appropriate set. If insertion is specified as manual then the user is responsible for connecting member records to the appropriate set by explicitly using the CONNECT statement.

The retention membership of a record may be specified as fixed, mandatory or optional. If the retention membership is specified as fixed then a record cannot be removed from the set. If the retention membership is specified as mandatory then a record can be removed from one set and logically reconnected to another. Only if the retention membership is specified as optional may the DISCONNECT statement be used to logically remove a member record from a set.

Statements to access database records
The basic retrieval and storage statements are GET, STORE, MODIFY and ERASE. The 'current record of the run unit' identifies the record referred to by the GET, STORE and ERASE statements. A FIND statement to identify the current record of the run unit must logically precede each of these statements.

The GET statement is used to fetch all or part of a database record into the user's work area. The MODIFY statement is used to write back the current record of the run unit when its contents have been amended. The ERASE statement logically removes the record identified by the currency indicator for the run unit from the database. If the record identified is an owner record then ERASE ALL will delete all member records and all descendants of the member records from the database. If the ALL option is not specified then the record can only be erased if the retention membership is specified as FIXED.

The STORE statement places a new record in the database; the currency indicator for the run unit will be modified to point to this new record. The other currency indicators will also be modified as appropriate unless the user specifies otherwise. The database record written by the STORE statement is created in the user's work area for the record type.

Record locks
To preserve the integrity of database records while allowing concurrent access by different programs, each record has two locks – a selection lock and an update lock. The locks are set by the database management system whenever a program accesses the record. The update lock is set when the contents of the record are modified or its set membership is changed.

If a record's update lock is set then no other program may access the record at the same time. The selection lock is set whenever a record is selected by a program. Several programs may select a record simultaneously, but when the selection lock is set no program may update the record. If the database key value for a record is placed on a keep list then the selection lock will remain set. The selection lock will remain until the database key is released from the keep list.

The remaining DML statements are READY, FINISH, ROLLBACK and COMMIT. The READY and FINISH statements are analogous to open and close statements in a conventional file system. The READY statement makes a realm ready for processing. Through the READY statement the user can indicate whether he intends to update records or simply to retrieve records. It can also be used to indicate whether the realm is to be shared or to be used exclusively. The user can specify that the realm can be shared by other users who wish to retrieve records but not to update. The FINISH statement indicates that the realm is no longer available. The ROLLBACK statement undoes all changes made to the database since the last quiet point. The COMMIT statement, as the name implies, commits all record changes to be made to the database and creates a quiet point. As a result of the COMMIT statement all keep lists are emptied and all record locks are released.

Exercises

Trophy	Racecourse	Date	Time	Horse	Owner	Trainer	Stable	Jockey	Odds	Distance		Weight
DB HANDICAP	CHEPSTOW	30/4	2.00	BAG OF BEANS	KERMIT	MISS PIGGY	MUPPET SHOW	FOZZY BEAR	10–1	3 miles	NH	10st 10lb
				GLAD RAGS	HERMIT	HOBO	PARK BENCH	A. TRAMP	50–1			9st 6lb
				DOBBIN	UGLY SISTERS	BUTTONS	CASTLE STABLES	PRINCE CHARMING	8–1			8st 12lb
RELATIONAL STAKES	CHEPSTOW	30/4	2.30	TRIGGER	ROY ROGERS	ANNIE OAKLEY	HOLLYWOOD	R. ROGERS	EVENS	2 miles	F	8st 7lb
				CLOTHES	WISHEY WASHEY	MRS MOP	LAUNDRY	MR BUN THE BAKER	100–30			8st 7lb
				VAULTING	WALTER	JIM	NASIUM	A. LEAPER	10–1			8st 7lb
				POMMEL	HANS	JIM	NASIUM	W. JUMPER	2–1			8st 2lb
DATA CUP	NEWMARKET	16/5	2.15	EEYORE	A.A. MILNE	PIGLET	THE WOLERY	CHRISTOPHER ROBIN	3–1	1 mile	F	9st 00lb
				HOBBY	RED KITE	PEREGRINE	THE EYRIE	MERLIN	EVENS			9st 00lb

Figure 67   *Racing database for Exercise 7.1*

7.1 Figure 67 represents a horse racing database.

(a) Normalize Figure 67 above into third normal form tables.

(b) Identify the queries that are likely to be made of the database.

(c) Decide which fields form the primary key fields for each table and which fields should have a secondary index.

(d) Write the IQL commands to determine the stable in which the horse GLAD RAGS is trained and the jockey who will ride the horse in the DB HANDICAP.

7.2 In club dinghy sailing cup competitions a record must be kept of the performance of each dinghy/helm combination for the series of races qualifying for the cup. There will be a separate cup for each class of dinghy. The database must record for each cup

The dinghies and helms competing
The class of the dinghy
The Portsmouth yardstick (handicap) of the dinghy
The date of each race
The position that the dinghy and helm came in each race.

(a) Draw a physical database record to represent the information in a hierarchical database.

(b) Choose a suitable storage structure for the records.

(c) Draw a data structure diagram to represent the information in a network database.

(d) Which pointers would you specify within the network database schema?

7.3 A photographer wishes to keep track of all photo assignments he undertakes. For each assignment he wishes to record the customer's name and where and when the photographs are taken. Each film is catalogued with a unique film serial number. The photographer may use several films on a single assignment, but a film may not contain photographs from more than one assignment. For each film the photographer records the make and type of film, the film speed and the development process used. For each photograph that he takes the photographer records the date and location, the aperture and shutter speed settings, the filter settings and exposure time used to print the negative.

When out on an assignment the photographer will often take photographs to file for future use. These photographs are to be classified by subject, e.g. landscape, candid, nature close-ups.

You are required to select which of the database approaches would be most appropriate, analyse the data and draw a suitable data structure diagram.

Part Three

Networks

8 Data communications

Communication terminology

This chapter describes the various modes of data transmission between one computer and another or between a computer and its terminals.

Parallel/serial transmission
Information is usually transmitted between devices as strings of characters. Each character will be represented by a code, usually a 6- or 8-bit code such as the ASCII (American Standard Code for Information Interchange) or EBCDIC (Extended Binary-Coded Decimal Information Code). The code to represent each character can be transmitted serially, the bits being transmitted one after another via a single connection. Alternatively the transmission may be in parallel, which means that each bit of the character code is transmitted simultaneously via a separate connection. Parallel transmission is normally reserved for connections which cover very short distances, owing to its prohibitive cost.

Simplex/half duplex/full duplex
These terms relate to the direction in which data may be transmitted. Simplex means that transmission is possible in one direction only. Its use is normally reserved for process control applications. For example, a heat sensor would be connected to a process control computer via a simplex line.

A half-duplex connection permits data to be transmitted in both directions but not simultaneously. While data is being transmitted in one direction control signals may be transmitted in the opposite direction. Changing the direction of transmission incurs a short delay while the line is switched. Half duplex is the normal mode by which a computer is connected to keyboard terminals.

Full-duplex connections permit simultaneous transmission in both directions and are used for intercomputer communications.

Synchronous/asynchronous transmission
Synchronization between the transmitting device and the receiving device is necessary at several levels (see discussion on protocols in Chapter 9).

The terms 'synchronous transmission' and 'asynchronous transmission' are used to describe the way in which synchronization may be achieved at the character level.

The receiving device must be able to identify the start and finish of each character transmitted. A character is transmitted as a pattern of bits, and to fail to correctly identify the start of a character could result in the data being misinterpreted.

Asynchronous transmission
In asynchronous transmission each character carries its own synchronization. Each character is framed by its own start and stop bits which identify the extent of the character. For example:

0	1 1 0 1 0 1 0 0	1 1
start bit	character code	stop bits

Between the transmission of characters, the line will transmit either a continuous stream of stop bits or nothing at all depending upon the bit level protocol. The presence of a single 0 bit will identify the start of a character. The start bit will be immediately followed by the bit pattern representing the character. The character will be terminated by one or two stop bits. If the speed of the line is given in bits per second (bps) then the start and stop bits must be taken into account when converting the line speed to characters per second (cps). For example, if each character requires eleven bits (i.e. one start bit, eight data bits, two stop bits) then a line speed of 110 bps is equivalent to 10 cps.

Asynchronous transmission is used extensively on slow keyboard terminals.

Synchronous transmission
In order to achieve higher transmission speeds, synchronization is established for a block of data. Each block of characters is preceded by a number of special synchronization characters:

SYN	SYN	SYN	SYN	data block

The size of the data block is determined by the buffer sizes of the devices being used and by the necessity to resynchronize transmission at frequent intervals.

The advantage of synchronous transmission is that data may be transmitted with very little overhead at the maximum speed of the line. It does require that terminals have their own buffers in which to build up messages for transmission and to receive messages.

Synchronous transmission is of particular advantage on shared lines as this minimizes the length of time for which a terminal requires use of the line.

Private/leased/switched lines

These terms govern the type of connection that is made between sending and receiving devices. The options that are available for the private user are:

1   To install a private line. The cost of a privately owned line is prohibitive over a long distance. However, once the line is installed the only further cost is for maintenance.

2   To lease a line from a public carrier. For example, British Telecom will lay a special cable or isolate existing spare channels to establish a permanent circuit between the sending and receiving devices. If a line is to operate in speeds in excess of 4800 bits per second then it is not possible to use lines isolated from the telephone network. (BT no longer has a monopoly in the UK as the public carrier.)

The cost of a leased line does not depend upon usage. There is an initial outlay to establish the link and a quarterly rental which is more than the usual telephone rental but is independent of usage.

The advantages of both leased and private lines are

(a)   High transmission speeds may be achieved.

(b)   There is no delay in establishing a connection.

(c)   There is no risk of making the wrong connection.

3   A switched line is an indirect connection between two stations. The connection is made via a network. There are two alternative possibilities: either a public or private telephone switching network, or a packet switching network. (A packet is a fixed size unit passed like a letter from exchange to exchange until it reaches its destination.) A telephone network is an example of a circuit switching network. When installing a private network the principal cost is in the purchase of the equipment. The charges for calls are based upon the duration of a call, the distance and the time of day. The cost of using a packet network depends upon the number of packets transmitted and is independent of how far they are transmitted.

Modulation

To achieve transmission over long distances then either the signal must be regenerated at regular intervals along the link or the signal must be modulated in such a way that 0 and 1 can still be distinguished. Transmission within the processor and over very short distances is achieved using DC signals; the binary values 0 and 1 are distinguished by having different voltage levels (-6 V and $+6$ V or 0 and 6 V). This representation is suitable for transmission over greater distances, but the signals must be regenerated at intervals of approximately a mile, as the resistance of the transmission line will cause the distinction between the two voltages to be lost. Transmission over long distances can alternatively be achieved by changing the amplitude, frequency or phase of a continuously alternating analogue signal. This signal is known as the carrier signal. The basic concepts of amplitude, frequency and phase modulation are explained below.

Amplitude modulation

The strength, or amplitude, of the signal may be altered. Two different amplitudes are used to distinguish 0 from 1 (Figure 68(a)).

Amplitude modulation is relatively inexpensive to implement but is very susceptible to interference occurring on the line.

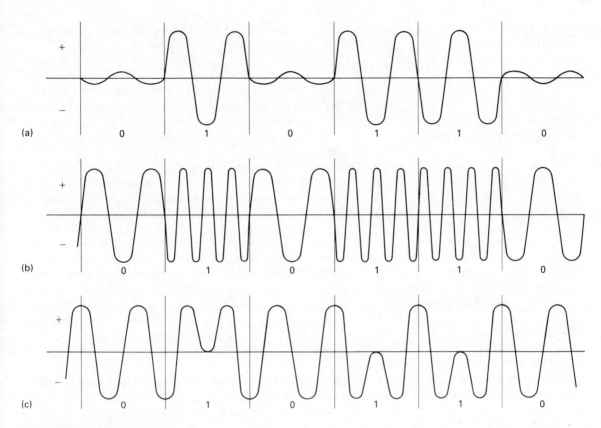

Figure 68   *(a) Amplitude modulation*
(b) Frequency modulation
(c) Phase modulation

Frequency modulation (frequency shift keying)
The frequency of the signal can be altered to distinguish 0 from 1 (Figure 68(b)).

Frequency modulation is less susceptible to interference and slightly more expensive than amplitude modulation.

Phase modulation
Phase modulation relies upon altering the phase of the signal. It is not the phase of the signal that is used to represent 0 and 1 but whether the phase changes. A phase change indicates a 1, and no change indicates 0 (Figure 68(c)).

Phase modulation is the least susceptible to interference but it is also the most expensive to implement.

Baud rate
The speed of a line is often measured in bits per second, but it may also be given as the number of bauds per second. The baud rate measures the number of 'signals' transmitted per second. In the simplest transmission systems each 'modulated signal' represents either 1 or 0 and the baud rate equals the number of bits per second. By combining two modulation techniques each modulated signal can be made to represent two bits of information; thus although the signal rate or baud rate remains the same, the effective number of bits per second is doubled.

Modems
The device used to convert binary digit values into modulated signals is called a modem.

'Modem' is an acronym derived from the words 'modulator' and 'demodulator'. The same device may be used to demodulate the signals, i.e. convert them back into binary digits.

Modems are available to operate at a variety of transmission speeds, from 200 bps to 72 000 bps. The maximum possible transmission speed over the public subscriber telephone network is 1200 bauds. For transmission speeds up to 1200 bps, frequency modulation is used, but with a modem using a combination of amplitude and phase modulation, a bit rate of 4800 bps can be achieved.

Higher speeds are only available on leased or private lines.

Modems operating at speeds less than 1200 bps transmit asynchronously, whereas modems operating at speeds greater than 1200 bps transmit synchronously. Synchronous and asynchronous modems are available to transmit at 1200 bps.

Digital transmission
Much of the data transmission traffic throughout the world is carried by the public telephone networks. The transmission of digital information using an analogue transmission network requires that the signals are modulated using one or more of the techniques described above. Digital trans-

mission has certain advantages over analogue transmission. It is more economic, and a signal that has become distorted can still be recognized and regenerated. The public telephone networks in several countries are changing over to digital transmission techniques. British Telecom hope to complete the changeover to System X, based upon digital transmission techniques, by the early 1990s.

Converting telephone networks to use digital transmission techniques means that speech patterns have to be modulated. The speech waveforms are turned into digital signals using a technique called *pulse code modulation* (PCM). The waveform is sampled 8000 times per second. Each sample is quantified and represented by a seven- or eight-bit number. A single speech channel produces 56 000/64 000 bits per second. A pulse code modulation system can handle a much faster data rate than this. In practice up to 32 channels can be multiplexed together to achieve a transmission rate of 2 megabits per second.

Figure 69 shows a speech waveform modulated using PCM. The quantified samples may be represented by sign and modulus or Excess 64/128 notation.

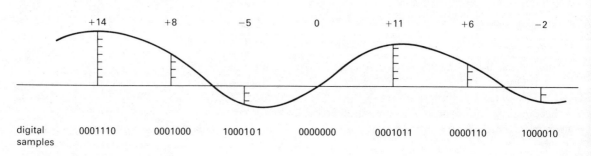

Figure 69   *Speech waveform using PCM*

Communication systems

Many of the concepts of data transmission are equally applicable to transmission between a peripheral device and the central processor and to transmission between different processors. A communication system can connect remote ter-

minals to a computer or interconnect computer systems.

The simplest method of connecting a terminal to a computer is to use a direct link. The direct attachment of a computer system to each terminal

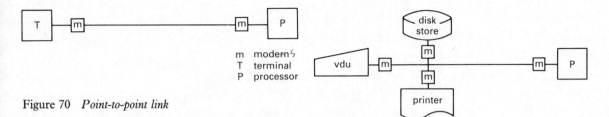

m   modem
T   terminal
P   processor

Figure 70   *Point-to-point link*

Figure 72   *Single remote job entry*

is termed point-to-point working (Figure 70).

Communication links are expensive, particularly over great distances. There are ways of reducing the cost. One technique is to use multipoint or multidrop working. With this technique several terminals can be connected to the same line (Figure 71).

The restriction upon this type of connection is that only one terminal may transmit or receive at a time. Each terminal must identify itself by a unique address when it transmits to the computer, and the computer must identify which terminal a message is destined for. Because the terminals cannot operate simultaneously, the computer must interrogate each in turn to see which are ready to transmit (see 'Polling' later in this chapter).

Multipoint working requires fewer modems than point-to-point working. Point-to-point working requires twice as many modems as there are terminals, whereas while multipoint working requires only one more modem than the number of terminals. There is, however, a reliability problem: a single modem or line failure can deny access to all the terminals connected to the line.

Multipoint working is suitable for applications where two or more terminals form a single remote job entry station (Figure 72). If the terminals are buffered and use synchronous transmission along a full duplex line then the users need hardly be aware that they are sharing the line.

The restrictions imposed by multipoint working can be avoided by using multiplexing techniques. A multiplexor is a device for enabling several terminals to transmit simultaneously along a communications link (Figure 73).

There are two commonly used techniques for allowing parallel use of the links. These are frequency division multiplexing and time division multiplexing.

Frequencing division multiplexors

A system using frequency modulation requires two different frequencies, to represent 1 and 0. Taking into account the fact that frequencies must be sufficiently different to easily distinguish between them, most links have a wide enough bandwidth to transmit several different frequencies. By allocating these frequencies in pairs to each terminal, several terminals may transmit simultaneously along the same line. This technique is known as frequency division multiplexing.

British Telecom offer twelve 110 bps channels from a single telephone link using frequency division multiplexing.

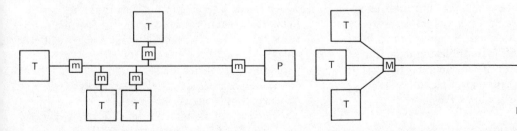

Figure 71   *Multipoint link*

M   multiplexor

Figure 73   *Multiplexor use*

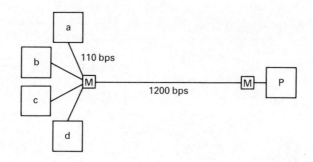

Figure 74   *Time slicing*

Time division multiplexors

If a number of slow-speed terminals are clustered together then the signals from these terminals may be multiplexed using a time slice technique (Figure 74). Time division multiplexing is achieved by transmitting one bit from each terminal in turn. The bit patterns from each terminal will be merged and transmitted in the sequence

$$a_1b_1c_1d_1a_2b_2c_2d_2a_3b_3c_3d_3 \ldots$$

The trunk line between the multiplexors operates at a much higher speed than the lines between the terminals and the multiplexor. The trunk line is capable of carrying the data to and from several terminals.

The maximum number of terminals that may be connected to the multiplexor is given by

$$\text{number of terminals} = \frac{\text{speed of trunk line}}{\text{speed of slow peripheral lines}}$$

In the example above

$$\text{number of terminals} = \frac{1200 \text{ bps}}{110 \text{ bps}} = 10$$

Multiplexors are usually supplied to handle 8 or 16 terminals. Time division multiplexing is extremely suitable for digital transmission systems. The established telephone network uses frequency division mutliplexing techniques. A rapid digitization of the telephone network to permit time division multiplexing should be completed by the early 1990s.

Statistical time division multiplexors
It is unlikely that all of the terminals connected to a multiplexor will wish to transmit simultaneously. Therefore, the trunk line will not be used to its full capacity. Statistical time division multiplexing (STDM) uses the trunk line more efficiently by allocating 'time slots' dynamically to terminals as they are required. The number of terminals transmitting simultaneously cannot exceed the capacity of the trunk line, although a greater number of terminals may be connected to a multiplexor.

The terminals transmitting must be identified to the receiving device; this means that the data transmitted by a terminal must be preceded by an identifying terminal number.

Concentrators
A concentrator is a device for sharing one or more output lines between several different input lines. It can connect several slow-speed asynchronous devices to a single high-speed trunk line, or it can be an exchange connecting several high-speed trunk lines. Packet switching and circuit switching exchanges, described in the next chapter, are examples of the second type of concentrator.

A concentrator has its own storage buffers in which the data received from the input lines is held. The contents of a buffer are transmitted when the appropriate output line becomes available.

Storage buffers may be dedicated to the connecting lines or allocated dynamically to messages as they arrive. If storage buffers are dedicated to individual lines then it is likely that inefficient use will be made of the available storage space, as transmission will be spasmodic.

Allocating buffers dynamically means that less storage space is required. The input lines have to contend for the available storage space.

Polling

Polling is a technique for determining which of a number of terminals is to transmit. For example, if several terminals are connected to a multipoint line such that only one terminal can transmit at a time, then the computer must ask each terminal in turn if it is ready to transmit. There are two different polling techniques.

Roll-call polling The computer maintains a list of all the terminals connected and sends a message to each terminal in turn enquiring whether it wishes to transmit. This approach can easily cope with changes in the terminal configuration caused by users logging on and off.

Hub polling The computer sends what is called a 'poll train' to one terminal. Each terminal in turn forwards the poll train to another terminal. The terminal in possession of the poll train is free to transmit a block of data, but having done so must forward the poll train. (Compare with token passing techniques, Chapter 10.) This technique requires more sophisticated terminal connections than roll-call polling.

Control of errors

If data is to be transmitted over any distance then the information is liable to be corrupted by signal distortion and noise on the line. Errors are more likely to occur during the transmission of data than in any other part of a computer system (assuming that the information itself was input correctly).

There are several approaches to the control of errors

Ignore the errors
Echo printing
Detection and retransmission
Error correcting codes

Ignoring errors

If the information being transmitted is text to be displayed upon a screen then the terminal operator can often allow for any errors by considering the corrupted text in context. Under these circumstances the effect of errors can be ignored. The terminal operator can usually request retransmission of any message not understood or repeat the operation. During data preparation sessions, the number of errors introduced by the operator makes the number of errors caused by transmission insignificant enough to be ignored.

Echo printing

A very simple error detection mechanism employed in many terminal-based systems is that of echo printing. This technique relies upon manual intervention to detect errors. Whatever the terminal operator types is not displayed immediately upon the screen but is transmitted directly to the central processor. The image that appears upon the screen is an 'echo' sent back from the line control unit attached to the central processor. If the image displayed disagrees with the character typed by the operator then an error has occurred. Unfortunately this error may have been introduced during the transmission of the echo.

Automatic error control

It is not possible to eliminate all errors, merely to make the occurrence of an error highly unlikely. The probability that an error will occur can be reduced to practically zero by using sophisticated transmission equipment. In order to control errors, it is first necessary to detect the presence of an error and then to make arrangements to correct it. Correction may be achieved by retransmitting the block of data containing the error (detection and retransmission) or by calculating what the data should have been (error correcting codes).

Detection and retransmission

Detection

The detection of errors is achieved by transmitting additional information which will be used by the receiving station to check the data. The transmitting station calculates check bits and then transmits both data and check bits. The receiving station uses the same calculation to decode the information as the transmitting station used to encode the data. Both stations should derive the same sequence of check bits. If the receiving station calculates a different set of check bits to those transmitted then it requests the transmitting station to retransmit the character or block. Two alternative techniques, parity checking and cyclic redundancy checking, are shown below.

Parity checking   The most straightforward technique for detecting errors is the addition of parity bits to the information transmitted. Parity may be odd or even. When odd parity is used then the number of 1s transmitted should always be odd; when even parity is used then the number of 1s should always be even. Parity may be added to an individual character or to a block of data.

For example, the ASCII code for T is 0010101 and the associated parity bit is 0 if odd parity is used because the number of 1s is already odd. Odd parity has the single advantage that the code 00000000 is never used.

Single parity will only detect an odd number of errors. If a single bit alters then the parity bit will be wrong, but if two bits change then the parity bit will still be correct.

Block parity may be used to increase the probability of detecting errors:

The final eight bits of the n character block will be entirely made up of column parity bits. This two-dimensional parity will not detect all errors but greatly reduces the probability of errors going undetected. It will detect all two-bit errors and most but not all four-bit errors.

Cyclic redundancy checking   One of the most efficient methods for detecting transmission errors is the use of cyclic (or polynomial) codes. The technique is based upon considering the information bits to be coded as the coefficients of a polynomial expression. For example, the bit pattern 1011001 would be considered as

$$1 \star x^6 + 0 \star x^5 + 1 \star x^4 + 1 \star x^3 + 0 \star x^2 + 0 \star x^1 + 1 \star x^0$$

The calculation of the check bits then takes place in stages:

1 Multiply the polynomial by x^n, which has the effect of shifting the bit pattern n places to the left and filling the least significant places with zeros.

2 Divide the polynomial expression by a unique divisor expression, which gives

$$\frac{\text{polynomial}}{\text{divisor}} = \text{quotient} + \frac{\text{remainder}}{\text{divisor}}$$

The highest term of the divisor must be x^{n-1}.

3 The message that is transmitted is the polynomial obtained in stage 1 with the trailing zeros replaced by the remainder calculated in stage 2.

The receiving station will make an identical calculation upon the polynomial and will compare the remainder calculated with that received from the transmitting station.

	b_0	b_1	b_2	b_3	b_4	b_5	b_6	row parity bit
1st data character	1	0	1	1	0	0	1	1
2nd data character	0	0	0	0	1	1	0	1
	.	.	.	.	.	.	.	.
	.	.	.	.	.	.	.	.
	.	.	.	.	.	.	.	.
nth data character	1	0	0	1	0	1	0	0
column parity bits	1	1	0	0	1	1	0	1

M-out-of-N-codes   The particular characteristic of *M*-out-of-*N*-codes is that *M* of the *N* bits used to represent each character are set to 1. Errors can be identified whenever the number of 1s is not equal to *M*. IBM make use of a four-out-of-eight code, which permits 70 valid combinations out of 256 possible combinations.

Retransmission

When an error is detected, the receiving terminal will request retransmission. The simplest approach is a stop–start transmission which requires an acknowledgement from the receiving station after each block of data. The receiving station will transmit either a positive acknowledgement (ACK) or a negative acknowledgement (NAK) after each block is received. The transmitting station will send the next block of data if it receives a positive acknowledgement or will retransmit the same block if it receives a negative acknowledgement. A limit is usually placed upon the number of times a block may be retransmitted. When this limit is reached the line may be assumed to be inoperable.

There will be a considerable time delay between the transmission of blocks of data as acknowledgement signals must be sent in the reverse direction. To avoid this delay a continuous stream of blocks of data can be transmitted, but this can cause problems in recovering from errors. The processing of the blocks will of course be behind the transmission of the blocks. By the time the transmitting station has been notified of an error, several further blocks of data will have been transmitted. The faster the line speed the greater the number of blocks transmitted. There are two alternative approaches to this problem. One is to retransmit all data blocks from and including the block in which the error was found. The second approach is to retransmit only the block in which the error was found, relying upon the receiving station to hold all blocks transmitted in the meantime. Both approaches require that the transmitting station has sufficient storage space to hold all blocks transmitted until acknowledgement has been received. The second approach also requires that the receiving station has similarly large buffers.

Error correcting codes

An alternative to retransmitting blocks of data after an error has been detected is to build sufficient redundancy into the code to enable the receiving station to correct the error. The technique of detecting and correcting errors using an error correcting code is known as 'forward error correction'.

The particular advantage of forward error correction is that the transmitting station does not have to store the blocks of data already transmitted as there is no retransmission of the data blocks which contain the errors. This means that a continuous stream of uninterrupted data can be transmitted.

An error correcting code can usually detect more errors than it can correct. For example, the Hamming code described below can detect single and double bit errors and can correct single bit errors. Hamming codes, which are among the best known error correcting codes, are based upon the use of parity check bits. Three parity bits are used to check four data bits.

The seven-bit code generated is transmitted in the following sequence (where bits p_1, p_2 and p_3 represent parity bits and d_1, d_2, d_3 and d_4 represent data bits):

$$p_1p_2d_1p_3d_2d_3d_4$$

Parity bit p_1 checks the parity of bits d_1, d_2 and d_4; parity bit p_2 checks the parity of bits d_1, d_3 and d_4; and parity bit p_3 checks the parity of bits d_2, d_3 and d_4. Odd parity is used for all parity bits. An example of the code (including parity bits) transmitted to represent the data pattern 0 1 1 0 would be:

0	0	0	1	1	1	0
p_1	p_2	d_1	p_3	d_2	d_3	d_4

However, if we suppose that the pattern received was

0	0	1	1	1	1	0
p_1	p_2	d_1	p_3	d_2	d_3	d_4

it can be easily seen that both parity bits p_1 and p_2 will now give the wrong parity. By considering the parity bits in reverse sequence we find that p_3 is correct and that p_1 and p_2 are incorrect:

$$p_3 \quad p_2 \quad p_1$$
$$\times \quad \times$$

If we represent a correct parity bit by 0 and an incorrect parity bit by 1, we have

$$p_3 \quad p_2 \quad p_1$$
$$0 \quad 1 \quad 1$$

This can be used as a binary value, from which we deduce that the third bit of the seven-bit code (d_1) is incorrect.

Exercises

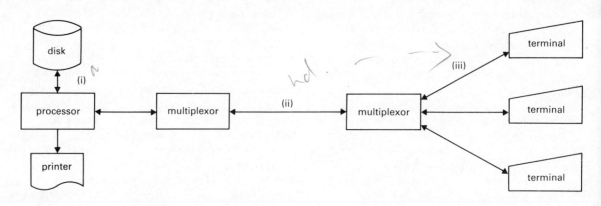

Figure 75   *Links for Exercise 8.1*

8.1   Decide whether the links (i), (ii), (iii) in Figure 75 should be

   (a)   Parallel or serial
   (b)   Simplex, half duplex or duplex
   (c)   Synchronous or asynchronous.

8.2   What is the difference between the baud rate and bits per second?

8.3   What is the difference between a multiplexor and a concentrator?

8.4   What would be the most suitable approach to handling errors in each of the following circumstances?
   (a)   Terminal used for program development connected to multiplexor
   (b)   Data entry terminal connected to minicomputer
   (c)   Magnetic tape drive connected to processor
   (d)   Transmission between processors
   (e)   Sensing device to process control microprocessor.

9   Computer networks

A network can serve two purposes. It may be used to connect computer systems in order to share processing capabilities, or it may be used to enable terminals to be connected to computer systems.

In network terminology the point at which several links coincide is called a node. The nodes may be computer systems to which the keyboard terminals are connected, or they may simply be exhanges which route messages between terminal stations. The terminal stations may be processors or keyboard terminals. Transmission is permitted between processors and between keyboard terminals and processors but not between keyboard terminals.

Circuit switching networks

In a circuit switched network, when two terminals wish to communicate a circuit is established between the terminals. This circuit connection is dedicated to the terminals until the call is finished (Figure 76). The circuit is established by making actual connections at each of the nodes on the route from A to C.

A connection established through the telephone network is sometimes referred to as a 'dial-up' line.

These lines are very susceptible to noise and interference as many of the switching stations are still mechanical. The digitization of the telephone network is intended to eliminate mechanical exchanges.

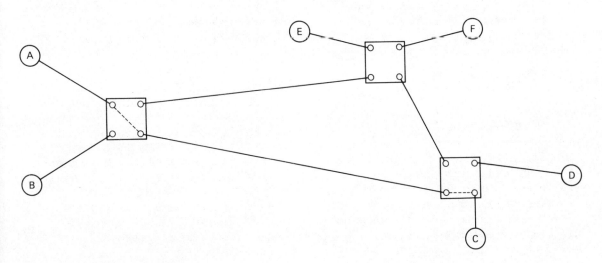

Figure 76   *Circuit switching network*

Packet switching networks

The objective of a packet switching network is to minimize the time that any single message spends in the network. To achieve this the messages, which may be of any size, are divided into fixed sized units called packets (Figure 77). A message is a logical, customer-defined unit, whereas a

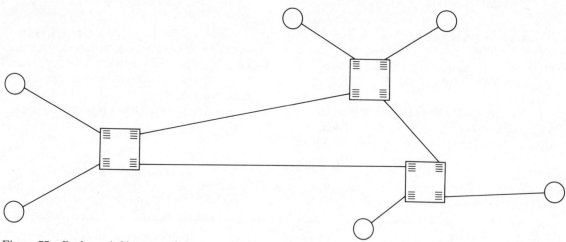

Figure 77   *Packet switching network*

packet is a physical system-defined unit. Each packet is transmitted to the nearest node in turn. The node will hold the packet until a connection to the next node in the route becomes free, at which point the packet is forwarded. Packets are transmitted only when a line becomes available.

On some systems it is possible for a terminal to broadcast the same message to several other terminals simultaneously. One of the characteristics of a packet switching network is that each of the links may operate at a different speed.

The forerunners of packet switching networks were message switching systems, first established in the 1920s. Complete messages were transmitted, which meant that the nodes had to have considerable storage capacity; this was achieved on the early systems using paper tape.

Network protocols

The purpose of a computer network is to enable users to communicate with remote computer systems. Users will require access to files, databases and programs stored throughout the network. The user may wish to make enquiries of the files or databases, communicate with other users, run programs or transfer material from one computer system to another. The user's terminal and the computer system must recognize each other's signals when transmission takes place; messages must be routed to their correct destinations; host operating systems must be able to control the communication services; and users must be able to perform a dialogue with remote computer systems. To achieve all of these requirements, protocols must be agreed to cover the communications network.

Protocols are a series of rules and procedures established to enable devices and systems to communicate with each other. Protocols are required at several different levels within a communications system. At the lowest level the protocol should govern the duration of and interval between bit signals; at the highest level it should control the transfer of programs and files. Figure 78 shows the seven layers of protocol for the reference model of open systems interconnection as defined by the International Standards Organization (ISO).

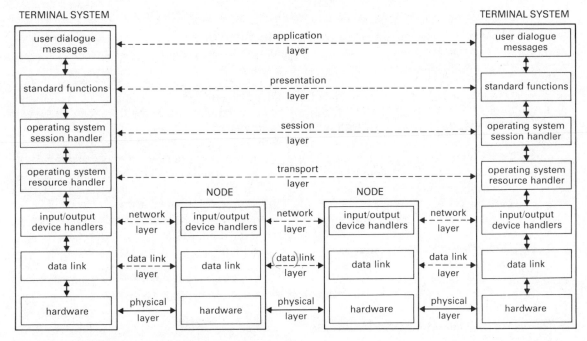

Figure 78 *ISO open systems interconnection reference model*

ISO reference model

The user's view of the communication system is a dialogue of messages between two terminals, shown by the dotted line labelled 'application layer' in Figure 78. The solid vertical lines show the actual interfaces that take place between each level. The solid horizontal lines show the physical communications that take place. The broken horizontal lines show the apparent communications that take place or how a user working at that level may view the system. The top four layers are end-to-end communication of messages; while the network layer deals with 'packets', the data link layer deals with blocks of data and the physical layer deals with strings of bits.

The operation of each layer should be transparent to the layers above. Each layer provides the basic services required by the higher layers. It should be possible to make changes at any level without it being apparent to the layers above.

Communication between devices only takes place at the physical level. No actual communication takes place between devices at higher levels, but each level interfaces to the level below using the functions and services provided by the lower level to achieve its own functions. This is why the functions of each layer overlap. The user's request may be interpreted as library requests which are, like all input/output requests, to be handled by the operating system. The operating system will invoke the appropriate device handlers which control the actual devices.

Physical layer

The physical layer is responsible for the transmission of bit patterns between devices. The recommendations for this level define such characteristics as the duration and voltage levels of the signals designed to represent 1 and 0. The definition of pin connections and transmission media are covered by these recommendations.

The recommendations cover point-to-point and multipoint configurations, serial and parallel connections, and half-duplex and full-duplex working.

Data link layer

The purpose of the data link layer is to provide

the network layer with an error-free transmission of data. The physical layer simply transmits a stream of bits which have no significance or meaning within the physical layer.

The data is arranged into blocks. Special bit patterns are used to indicate the start and end of each block. Care must be taken to ensure that if these special bit patterns should occur within the data they cannot be interpreted as start or stop bit patterns. This is achieved by a technique called *bit stuffing* (described below). The data link layer is also responsible for ensuring that transmission is error free and, if necessary, retransmitting the block of data (see 'Control of errors' in Chapter 8).

If data is to be transmitted as a continuous stream of blocks then the data link layer must ensure that the transmitting station does not send data faster than the receiving station can deal with it.

The data link layer is also responsible for ensuring that blocks are neither lost nor duplicated.

Bit stuffing is a technique for preventing specific bit patterns occurring naturally within the data. A significant pattern such as 11111110 will be chosen as the start block control character. If any string of seven or more 1s occurs naturally in the data then the transmitting device inserts an extra 1 bit. The receiving device will remove one 1 from every string of more than seven 1s. The receiving device can then treat every string of exactly seven 1s as a start block control character.

Network layer

Messages must be formed into packets for transmission; this task is performed by the network layer. The network layer is responsible for ensuring that these packets are then correctly routed to the destination node. The important functions of the network layer are:

To select the route for the packet
To prevent the network from becoming congested
To ensure that packets arrive in the correct sequence

Transport layer

The transport layer is the lowest level responsible for source-to-destination communications. The lower levels all work from node-to-node (see Figure 78). The transport layer is responsible for identifying the processes being connected. Many of the computers will be multiprogramming, so the transport layer must establish a connection with the appropriate program or process.

The services of the network layer and the transport layer can overlap. If the transmission of packets from node to node is governed by a virtual circuit protocol, then the network layer will be responsible for forming the messages into packets. If the transmission service is provided by a datagram protocol, then the transport layer provides a packet assembly/disassembly facility.

The transport layer determines the service provided to the session layer:

Virtual circuit service   Messages are transmitted with a guaranteed error-free delivery.
Datagram service   Single packets are transmitted with no guarantee of the order in which the packets will be delivered or of an error-free delivery.
Broadcast service   The same message may be transmitted to several destinations.

Session layer

The session layer is essentially the user's interface with the network. It is through the session layer that the user establishes contact with a process in another machine and then carries on a dialogue.

The session layer is responsible for setting up a session. This firstly involves establishing the right of the two parties to communicate with each other, e.g. a user may be attempting to access a secure database for which he has no authority. The session layer will also establish the nature of the interaction, i.e. full duplex, half duplex or simplex.

The session layer is responsible for ensuring the continuity of the dialogue. If a line or node failure should break the connection, then the session layer must re-establish the call in such a way that the user need never know it was broken.

However, it is not always feasible to re-establish a connection. This could leave a file or database partially updated. In most systems it is important that the database should not be left in an inconsistent state. To avoid this the session layer may 'quarantine' the data. This means that although some data may have arrived at the destination node, it is not released to the destination process until all the data has arrived.

The functions of the session and transport layers can be combined into a single level.

Presentation layer
The purpose of the presentation layer is to eliminate the incompatibility between the transmitting and receiving terminals and the character sets used by different machines. Terminals differ in many respects, such as the number of lines on a screen, or the width in characters of a printer. It is the presentation layer at either end of a communication link that makes allowance for these discrepancies.

The presentation layer will also perform code-to-code conversions to make allowance for different machine codes. File formats also differ between machines, and these can be compensated for in the presentation layer.

In many applications particular keywords occur frequently. These keywords can often be coded to reduce transmission time. This function can also be built into the presentation layer.

Application layer
The dialogue between a user and a process at the application level is really determined by the author of the process. At this time there are no agreed protocols to cover the application layer.

Agreed standards
The ISO reference model for open systems interconnection is a recommendation for the seven levels of protocols that should be agreed. Standard protocols have been agreed for the three lower levels, although of course standards can only be recommended and many networks have been in existence longer than the standards. The recommended standards for the physical layer are CCITT recommendations V28, X24 and X21 covering the electrical, functional and procedural connections respectively. At the data link level the ISO standard HDLC (high-level data link control) has been generally accepted, and at the network level CCITT recommendation X25. The CCITT recommendation covers all three levels by specifying X21 and HDLC for the lower levels.

High-level data link control
The high-level data link control (HDLC) proposals cover the error-free transmission of blocks or frames of data. The proposals cover the format of an HDLC frame and the control of traffic between stations at the data link level. The proposals require that one of the stations is responsible for controlling the flow of data; this is the primary station. The frames transmitted by the primary station are referred to as the *command frames*. The frames transmitted by the secondary station are referred to as the *response frames*. If one intelligent station is connected to several very simple terminals then the intelligent terminal must be the primary station in order that it may control the link. If two intelligent terminals are connected then either terminal may assume the responsibility for controlling the link and become the primary station.

The format of an HDLC frame is:

flag	address	control signals	information Data	frame check sequence	flags

The exchange of frames between stations may take place in one of the following ways:

Normal response mode Secondary stations may only respond when they have been polled by a primary station.
Asynchronous response mode Either primary or secondary stations may transmit when they detect that the link is idle.
(Either of the above modes may be used when several secondary stations are connected to the same primary station.)
Balanced mode For the connection of two intelligent terminals either of which may assume the role of the primary station.

The flags

The flags are unique bit patterns used to indicate the start and end of a frame. The bit sequence 01111110 is defined in the HDLC standards as the unique pattern used as start and end flags. If a bit sequence of six or more 1s occurs naturally then a zero bit is inserted after the fifth one. For example,

    0111111110   becomes   01111101110
    and   01111110   becomes   011111010

When a sequence of consecutive 1s is received the length of the string is significant; a 0 following five 1s is discarded; a 0 following six 1s is treated as a flag sequence; and a 0 following seven or more 1s signifies that the tranmission of the frame has been aborted.

Address field *(8 bits)*

The address field in a command frame (one transmitted by the primary station) contains the address of the destination (secondary) station. The address field in a response frame contains the address of the station replying, which is again that of the secondary station.

A station may have more than one address; one address must be unique, but the others may be shared by several stations. These shared addresses are called group addresses, and frames containing a group address will be received by all the stations in the group.

Control field *(8 bits)*

There are three different control field formats defined in the HDLC proposals. These definitions cover information frames for the transmission of data, supervisory frames used to control the flow of data, and unnumbered frames which are used to control the link.

Information frames   Each of the information frame control fields contains a send sequence number and a receive sequence number. A station can use these fields to confirm that the send sequence number corresponds with the number of frames that the station has received and that the receive sequence number corres-

ponds with the number of frames that it has transmitted.

The information field may be of any length, though it is usually based upon an exact number of characters.

Supervisory frames   Used to perform supervisory functions such as

> Acknowledge a previously received information frame
> Indicate that a station is ready to receive an information frame
> Indicate that a station is busy and not in a position to receive further information frames
> Request retransmission of a particular frame or of all frames following a specified frame

Supervisory frames, like information frames, contain sequence numbers.

Unnumbered frames   Used to control the link. They are used to perform functions such as

> Establish the link mode (i.e. normal response mode, asynchronous response mode or balanced mode)
> Disconnect a link (this can only be transmitted by a primary station; a secondary station must send a request disconnection frame)
> Acknowledge an unnumbered frame
> Indicate that an invalid frame has been received

Frame check sequence *(16 bits)*

When a frame is transmitted the frame check sequence is calculated using a cyclic redundancy check (see Chapter 8) with a polynomial divisor of

$$x^{16} + x^{12} + x^5 + x^0$$

The same calculation is performed when the frame is received. If the frame check sequence is incorrect, the frame is rejected.

The length of the information field is not defined, so the frame check sequence is taken to be the sixteen bits immediately preceding the end of frame flag.

HDLC dialogue

To establish a link the primary station transmits an unnumbered frame to set the required

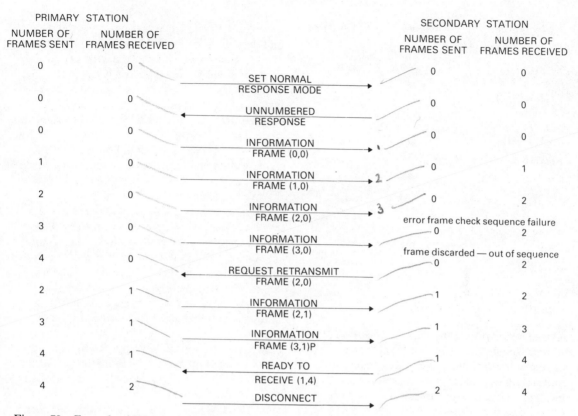

Figure 79 *Example of HDLC dialogue*

response mode. The secondary station acknowledges with an unnumbered response. The primary station is then free to transmit the first of the information frames. In the example in Figure 79 the primary station transmits two information frames successfully but the third frame fails the frame sequence check. This frame and the one following will be discarded. The secondary station requests that both frames are retransmitted. When the primary station retransmits the fourth information frame it specifically requests an acknowlegement from the secondary station (indicated by P). The secondary station uses a supervisory frame to acknowledge that the frame was successfully received and that the station is ready to receive further frames. The primary station, however, disconnects the link.

Packet level control

The following description is based upon the X25 recommendations for a packet level protocol (Figure 80).

When one terminal wishes to establish a virtual circuit between itself and another terminal, then the terminal wishing to make contact sends a *call request packet* to the node of the network to which it is attached. The call request packet is delivered by the network to the destination terminal. If the called terminal is in a position to accept the connection, it returns a *call accepted packet*. The called terminal may not be able to accept the call for a variety of reasons: the terminal may be busy or it may be part of a closed user group to which the calling terminal is prohibited access. In these circumstances a *clear request packet* is returned. If the terminal being called fails to respond at all, then after a suitable time-out period (typically 200 seconds) the network will return a clear request packet.

When the original calling terminal has received

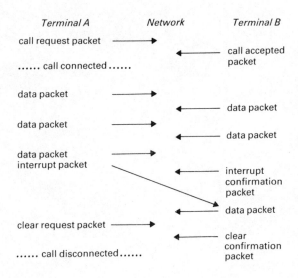

Figure 80   *Packet level protocol*

a call accepted packet then it is in a position to transmit the first data packets. From then on both terminals are free to transmit data packets or to terminate the connection. To break a connection one of the terminals transmits a clear request packet; the other terminal on receipt returns a *clear confirmation packet.*

Each data packet header includes a sequence number. This sequence number is used as a check on the packets transmitted between the terminal and the node to which it is connected and vice versa. If either station detects a break in the sequence then it knows that a packet has been lost. Confirmation that a packet has reached its destination can be requested by setting a single bit in the packet header. This is responded to by the receiving station, but can be complicated if the sending and receiving terminals have different packet sizes.

A transmitting terminal is limited in the number of packets it may send to the receiving terminal. When this limit has been reached the transmitting terminal is prohibited from sending any further packets until it receives a *receive ready packet* from the receiver. The receiving station can, however, transmit a *receive not ready packet* which prevents the transmitting station from sending any more packets until a receive ready packet is received.

These restrictions do not apply to the transmitting of an *interrupt packet.* An interrupt packet has priority over *data packets* and will be transmitted in advance of any data packets waiting to be transmitted. When the interrupt packet has been delivered the receiving terminal will respond with an *interrupt confirmation packet.*

Network topology

The design of a network is based upon two criteria

1   The positioning of the exchanges or nodes
2   The interconnection of the nodes.

The routing strategy and, in particular, the response and delay times will be affected by the choice of network topology. Any mistakes made in the design of the network can be very expensive and difficult to rectify.

The design constraints of public networks will be different from those of private networks. In a private network the location and much of the detail relating to prospective traffic can be determined before the network is designed.

Routing is based upon known traffic. A company wishing to install a private network to interconnect several sites has the choice of positioning the exchanges at the existing sites or of purchasing new sites to house the exchanges.

With a public network, the eventual number of customers and the volume and nature of traffic can only be estimated when the network is designed. The presence of the network itself will invite traffic. A public carrier must position the nodes of the network in such a way as to provide as large a catchment area as possible. A subscriber is more likely to make use of a network if the exchanges are conveniently positioned. The designers of a public network must avoid congestion without any real knowledge of the eventual traffic.

The eventual network may be based upon one of the following topologies or designed as a combination of the various techniques.

Distributed networks

In a distributed network (Figure 81) each node is connected to two or more other nodes. There are several alternative routes through a network. The route taken by a packet is selected by a routing algorithm. If any line or node on the chosen route fails then one of the alternative routes can be selected. The routing algorithm will be designed to avoid the possibility of packets looping (see below) within the network. Most public service networks have a distributed topology.

If the routing strategy chosen causes a packet to be returned to a node that has already received this packet, then this is termed *looping*. A special case of looping occurs when a packet is returned along the path on which it arrived; the packet is then in danger of oscillating between the two nodes, termed *ping-ponging*.

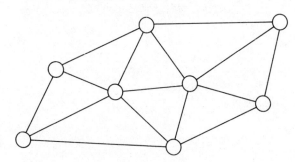

Figure 81   *Distributed network*

Star networks

A star network (Figure 82) is the simplest network to set up. Each terminal node is connected to a single exchange. Star networks are generally limited to local applications because of the prohibitive cost of long transmission lines. The network relies heavily upon the central exchange and is susceptible to failure. No routing algorithm is necessary, and looping and ping-

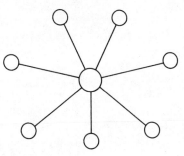

Figure 82   *Star network*

ponging cannot occur. The network is very easy to extend up to the capacity of the exchange.

Satellite networks

A satellite network (Figure 83) is a particular case of a star network. Satellite networks are ideal for the interconnections of international networks; distance is of little importance, and the alternative may be ocean bed cables. Satellite networks are suitable for broadcasting and conference systems. Expansion is limited to the number of terminals that can be handled by the satellite.

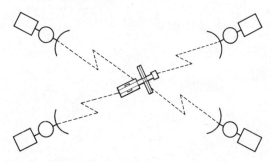

Figure 83   *Satellite network*

Ring networks

In a ring network (Figure 84) each terminal is a link in a chain. The chain is joined at both ends to form a complete circle. There is no routing algorithm; all traffic is directed around the ring. The source node places the packet on the ring and each node in turn examines the packet. The destination node extracts the packet, marks it as received and returns it to the ring to be picked up by the source node. All other nodes forward the packet.

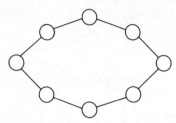

Figure 84   *Ring network*

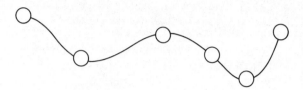

Figure 85   *Bus network*

The reliability of a ring network can be improved by connecting each node to two other nodes in each direction. A single node or line failure does not then completely destroy the ring. Ring network topology is favoured by local area networks. In local area networks, each node has a repeater station powered from the ring to forward packets when the node is switched off. Rings are susceptible to the failure of a single critical component.

Bus networks

Each node in a bus network (Figure 85) is connected to a single channel. This design is used in many local area networks (see 'Ethernet' Chapter 10). The network can be thought of as an open-ended ring. Each node is a link in the chain, but the chain does not form a complete loop. The connection of a node to the bus can be made in such a way that if the node fails it does not break the network. However, a single line failure can split the network. A combination of bus networks can be used to build a tree-structured network.

Packet radio networks

Packet radio networks use radio transmitter/ receivers to connect terminals with exchanges, making connections which could not have been achieved as cheaply using land-based links. The first application of a packet radio network was to connect the outlying Hawaiian Islands to the University of Hawaii computer centre. The Hawaiian greeting *aloha* has subsequently been used to describe this type of network. Sea-bed cables or satellite links are more expensive alternatives to radio connections.

Routing and congestion can become a problem within this type of network, particularly when local atmospheric conditions cause packets to be lost or corrupted by interference. The protocol used has to cope with the increased probability of lost or corrupted packets.

There is no problem in introducing extra terminals providing that the number of terminals remains within the capaity of the network. This type of network will easily support mobile terminals.

Routing of packets

In a packet switching network the packet can traverse the network by many different paths. Selecting the route to be taken by a packet is a function of the network layer. The route taken will be determined by the routing strategy.

Many different routing strategies have been proposed, but not all have been implemented. The choice of strategy will depend upon the following criteria:

1   The simplicity with which the strategy can be implemented.
2   The adaptability of the chosen strategy to changes in the volume of traffic.
3   The resilience of the strategy to failure within the network.

Each node uses a routing table to determine the link through which to forward a packet. The routing table contains one entry for every other node in the network, indicating which of the links connected to the node should be used to forward a packet. The contents of the routing table may be fixed or may be updated to respond to prevailing conditions. The updating of the routing table may be performed by the node itself or by a central routing supervisor.

If there is more than one possible route between two nodes then the route may be calculated for each packet or it may be determined for the duration of a session. (See 'Virtual circuits and datagrams', later in this chapter.)

The routing strategy will have a profound effect upon the response time experienced by a user at a terminal, so network designers have to consider carefully which strategy they are going to use. It is not easy to change the routing strategy once a network has been installed.

Fixed routing
The route taken by packets between two given terminals will always be the same. The route is predetermined and the only way of applying alterations is by operator or program intervention. Using fixed routing, delay times can be very long as the strategy cannot respond to variations in traffic flow. If a node or line fails then some terminals will be isolated from the rest of the network.

Alternative routing
Alternative routing is a variation upon fixed routing. Each node holds in its routing tables a single alternative path by which a packet may be delivered. The alternative route will be selected if the primary link is not available due to a fault or congestion. This technique is slightly better than fixed routing, but is only really suitable for small networks. Alternative routing should be able to cope with a single line or node failure; but in a large network, if the alternative routes have not been selected carefully, packets could loop indefinitely.

Random routing
When a packet arrives at a node, the link along which the packet will be forwarded is selected at random. The final destination is not taken into account. This technique can result in packets being transferred in completely the wrong direction and is likely to produce excessive response times. However, the system can adapt well to line and node failures.

Queue length routing
The route selected for a packet is along the link with the shortest queue. The selection is made regardless of the eventual destination of the packet. This is not a very suitable basis for calculating the route as the packet may be transmitted in completely the wrong direction (even if the packet is prevented from being transmitted along the link on which it arrived). This algorithm can be a suitable basis for calculating which of a number of possible alternative links to use if the primary route is congested.

The above algorithms are extremely easy to implement and therefore the implementation cost is likely to be low. It is possible to implement all of the above algorithms using hardware. The remaining algorithms take into account changes in conditions within the network, although they do not all consider the source or destination involved.

Distributed adaptive routing
The ARPANET algorithm
The ARPANET routing algorithm is one of the category of strategies described as distributed adaptive algorithms. (ARPANET: Advanced Research Projects Agency Network, now Defence Advanced Research Projects Agency.) This means that each node updates its own routing tables using information received from each of the nodes to which it is connected. Each node transmits a packet of delay times to each of its immediate neighbours at frequent intervals (typically 2/3 s). A node will calculate its network delay table from the delay times it receives from its neighbours.

The network delay table is used to calculate the optimum link via which to forward a packet. Consider a node, say node F in Figure 86, which has three links to other nodes. Its network delay table could be as follows:

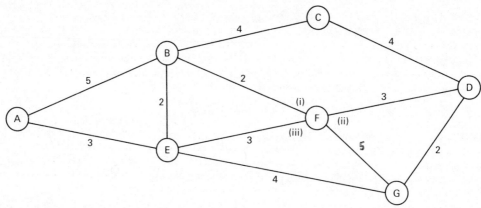

Figure 86   *ARPANET routing*

Link	Node						
	A	B	C	D	E	F	G
(i)	7	2	6	10	4	-	8
(ii)	12	11	7	3	9	-	5
(iii)	6	5	9	9	3	-	7

The values in the table are estimates of the time taken for a packet to reach a node along a particular link. From its network delay table, a node can calculate the minimum delay time to reach any other node:

minimum delay table

node	A	B	C	D	E	F	G
time	6	2	6	3	3	–	5

These delay times are passed to each of node F's immediate neighbours, which are also transmitting packets of minimum delay times at regular intervals. Suppose that node F receives the following revised table from node D:

A	B	C	D	E	F	G
9	5	2	–	6	3	2

From node F's knowledge of the time taken to reach node D it can revise its own entry for link (ii) in the network delay table:

	A	B	C	D	E	F	G
link (ii)	12	8	5	3	9	–	5

From the revised network delay table the node can revise its own minimum delay time packet.

The basis of this algorithm is to transmit each packet along the estimated shortest path. The less time a packet spends in the network, the less it can contribute to congestion. The algorithm responds quickly to any reductions in delay time, but slowly to failures or increases in delay time. The minimum delay time packets transmitted at frequent intervals generate a considerable overhead in traffic.

If a network is to be extended, then the routing tables for every other node must be changed.

Backward-learning routing algorithm
The backward-learning routing algorithm, like the ARPANET routing algorithm, relies upon information from other nodes in the network to keep its routing tables up to date. Unlike the ARPANET algorithm, the backward-learning algorithm does not send explicit delay times packets. Instead the backward-learning algorithm relies upon updating its routing tables from information carried in data packets that pass through the node.

Each packet is time stamped by the source node. Every node that receives the packet calculates the time taken for the packet to reach it and uses this information to update its routing table.

The drawbacks to this approach are that traffic between nodes can be spasmodic, which means that the routing table may not be up to date and that the delay times are all calculated using packets travelling in the opposite direction to the packets that will be transmitted.

Centralized routing

The route to be taken by a packet between the source and destination node is calculated by a central supervisory node. The algorithm is designed to calculate the optimum route between any two nodes, and the route selected is established as a virtual circuit for the duration of a session. The central supervisory node responds to information it receives periodically from every other node. The transmission of this information to and from the central supervisory node can result in congestion on the links leading to and from the supervisory node.

To establish a virtual circuit, the source node informs the central supervisory node of the destination. The central supervisory node computes the best route, based upon line capacities and queue lengths, and then sends a message to every node along the selected route to set up an entry in its routing table and to reserve buffers for the virtual circuit. When each of the nodes has returned an acknowledgement, the central supervisory node informs both the source and destination nodes that the virtual circuit has been established.

The algorithm establishes the best route according to the conditions prevailing when the circuit is initiated. The route is not changed if the prevailing conditions should change unless a failure actually breaks the circuit. The efficiency of this algorithm depends upon the rate at which traffic volume changes. The algorithm can take into account under-utilized regions of the network when establishing routes.

The central supervisory node is a critical component of the network and, if it should fail, no virtual circuits can be established. A solution to this is to incorporate standby supervisors into the network. Under normal operating conditions these act as ordinary nodes, but if the central supervisory node should fail then one of the standby supervisors can be activated. Although the network topology may be a distributed network, the control structure must be that of a tree. When a new supervisor assumes control it must determine the current state of the network and establish its own tree. It can only do this by interrogating every other node in the network.

If a link or node fails within the tree, then part of the tree may be lost. The supervisor has to regain control of as many nodes as possible through alternative branches of the tree. The control tree structure of the network is therefore dynamically changing.

Delta routing

Delta routing uses a central supervisory node to calculate the optimum route between every pair of nodes at periodic intervals, but the choice of the actual route through which to forward a packet is left to the individual node.

There will be a number of links connected to each node. The central supervisory node will calculate the estimated time to reach every other node along each of the links. It will inform each node which is the optimum link through which to forward a packet to each of the other nodes. Alternative links are deemed to be equivalent to the best route if the time taken to reach the destination node along that link differs from the best route by less than a quantity 'delta'. In Figure 87, the times to reach node F from node A are as follows:

Along link (i)	7.6 s
Along link (ii)	7.4 s
Along link (iii)	7.2 s

The times are the delay times for packets travelling through the network from node A to node F. The shortest route is via link (iii). Depending upon the value of delta, other links will be considered to be 'equivalent' to this best link; for example, if delta = 0.3 s then link (ii) will also be considered to be an optimum link.

Node A will make its own selection along which of the optimum links to forward a packet, based upon local prevailing conditions.

Hierarchical routing tables

The routing table for each exchange should contain one entry for every other node in the network, indicating the link through which to

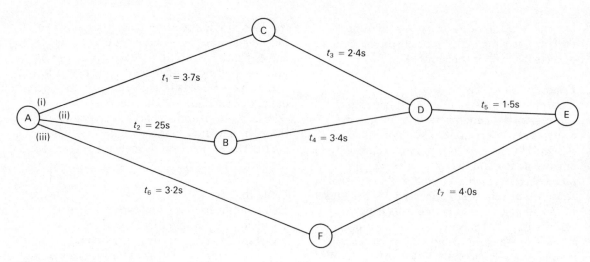

Figure 87   *Delta routing*

forward packets destined for that node. If there are a great number of exchanges then the table will be very large. The size of the table can be reduced by subdividing the network into regions. One node in each region will act as a port for all packets passing to and from that region. The packet destination address will identify the port to the destination region, and a secondary address will identify the destination node within the region.

The table will be constructed as two parts. One part contains an entry for each of the other nodes within the same region. The second part contains one entry for each of the ports to other regions.

If the network is exceptionally large then the regions themselves may be subdivided. The fact that all traffic between regions must pass along the link connecting the regions can result in heavy traffic along these particular links. Hierarchical routing is used to connect international networks.

Routing in packet radio networks

Broadcast or flooding routing algorithm
In broadcast routing (Figure 88) every packet is given a unique identifier and a count of the number of hops necessary for it to reach its destination. The source node will broadcast the packet. Each node that receives the packet will store the packet identifier in its transmission

table, decrement the hop count and retransmit the packet. In this way the packet will be propagated through the network. The destination node will identify packets intended for it by the identifier carried in the packet header.

If the hop count of a packet arriving at a node is zero then the packet will not be retransmitted. This ensures that the packet will never travel further than the maximum number of hops in any direction.

When a node transmits a packet then some of the adjacent nodes will receive the packet for a second time. A node that finds a packet identifier already in its transmission table will treat this as an acknowledgement message and should not retransmit the packet. Looping of packets can be controlled by the use of the transmission tables and the hop counts. Broadcast routing is very inefficient but it can be used where the nodes are also mobile.

Distributed broadcast routing algorithm
The distributed broadcast routing algorithm operates upon a similar basis to the ARPANET algorithm. Every node has a distance vector which gives the number of hops between itself and every other node (Figure 89).

Node C transmits a packet destined for node F. Included in the header of the packet will be its

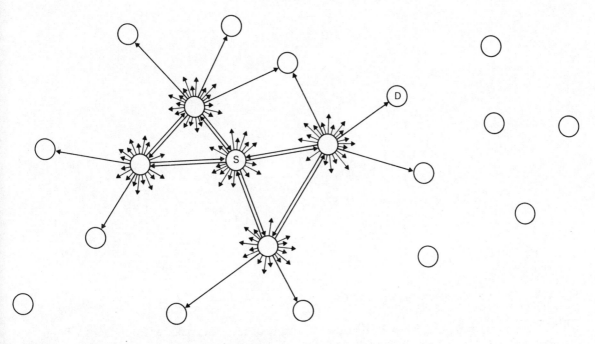

Figure 88 *Broadcast routing. The destination node D is only two hops away from the source node S*

destination F and the distance from the transmitting node to the destination. The packet will be received by nodes A, B and D, each of which will examine its own distance vector to find the

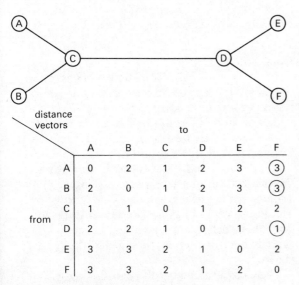

Figure 89 *Distributed broadcast routing*

distance vectors

		to					
		A	B	C	D	E	F
from	A	0	2	1	2	3	③
	B	2	0	1	2	3	③
	C	1	1	0	1	2	2
	D	2	2	1	0	1	①
	E	3	3	2	1	0	2
	F	3	3	2	1	2	0

number of hops to F. Only terminal D has a lower value than that in the header.

Terminal D will decrement the distance in the header and broadcast the packet. Terminal F can recognize that the packet is intended for it by the fact that the entry in the distance vector is zero.

The algorithm allows direct communication between any two nodes. If there is a path to the destination then the packet will find it. The main disadvantages are that the packet might be duplicated and there is a need to maintain an updated set of distance vectors.

Hierarchical routing algorithm
The hierarchical routing algorithm takes into account the fact that there are two different types of node. These are

Switching centres which are associated with the processing capabilities of the network
Repeaters which simply accept and forward packets.

In other words the distinction between exchanges and processors is recognized. Most of the traffic

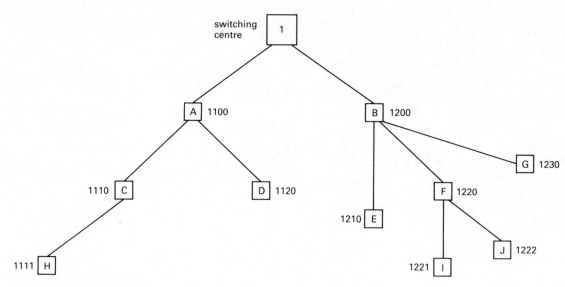

Figure 90   *Hierarchical routing to a single switching centre*

within the network will be between the repeaters (associated with the exchanges) and the switching centres (associated with the processors). Any traffic between exchanges can be forced through a switching centre.

The repeater nodes can be thought of as forming part of a hierarchical structure. Each repeater will be assigned a label which reflects the structure. See Figure 90.

A label can be used as an address for the transmission of packets in both directions. A repeater node is said to be at level n in the hierarchy if the first n fields of the label are non-zero. A repeater station can forward a packet *en route* to the switching centre by replacing the nth digit of the label by zero and retransmitting the packet. For example, repeater F (label 1220) is at level 3 and so it can adjust the label to 1200 and forward the packet.

A repeater node that receives a packet *en route* from the switching centre will only accept the packet if the first n fields of the packet identifier correspond with the repeater's label.

There will be a separate hierarchical routing structure for each switching centre (Figure 91). The repeater node will have a separate label for each tree structure. The repeater station will place the labels in a table in order of priority based upon the distance of the repeater from the switching centre.

The advantages of hierarchical routing are:

1   The algorithm allows shortest-path routing between repeaters and switching centres.
2   Packets have a high probability of reaching their destinations.
3   The labels and structure can be updated in the event of failure or congestion.
4   Only one node need respond to a packet.

Congestion

Congestion occurs when the number of packets in one part of the network exceeds the volume of traffic that can be handled by the nodes. Each node will have buffers in which to hold a number of packets waiting to be processed or transmitted. Congestion is likely to occur if the buffers become full. If the input buffers of one node become full then the node cannot accept any more packets. As a consequence, packets will queue up waiting to transmit to this node and congestion will spread through the network. Congestion leads to a degradation of the service provided by the network.

There are several ways of combating congestion:

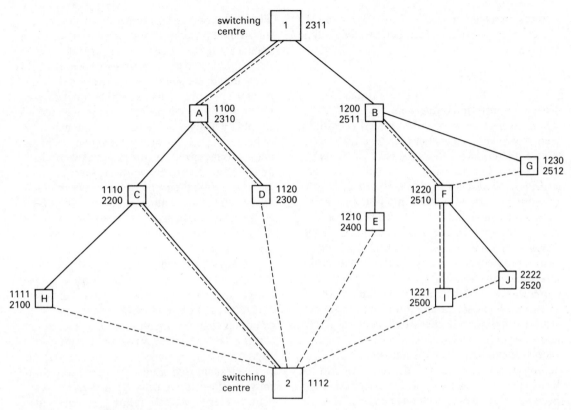

Figure 91 *Hierarchical routing to two switching centres*

To prevent it occurring If the routing of packets is determined by a central supervisory node then the virtual circuit will be established for the duration of a session. Buffers will be reserved at each node along the route. Congestion will not occur as storage space is reserved for each virtual circuit. Buffers reserved for permanent virtual circuits will be unused for much of the time and represent an inefficient use of resources.

To discard any packets that arrive once the buffers are full No packet should be discarded without first being examined. The incoming packet could be an acknowledgement packet, indicating that a previously transmitted packet has arrived successfully. The packet will have been stored until the acknowledgement arrives, so the buffer space occupied by the packet can now be released. If the incoming packet is intended to be forwarded to another node then

it will be discarded. The transmitting node will eventually retransmit the packet if it receives no acknowlegement.

Isarithmic control This policy is based on maintaining the same number of packets within the network at all times. There are two slightly different approaches. In the first, all packets must be kept circulating, which means that a node must wait for an empty packet frame to arrive before it may introduce a new packet into the network. The second approach allows a node to hold on to a number of packets. These may be packets queuing for a particular link or empty packet frames awaiting use. There will be a limit to the number of packets a node may hold. If a packet arrives at a node which already holds its quota of packets then the node should dispatch an empty packet frame to any other node at random. A packet can only enter the network if the source node has an empty packet frame in which to place it. Isarithmic control cannot ensure that localized congestion will not occur.

Virtual circuits and datagrams

The network layer protocol is concerned with the transmission of packets between terminals. The protocol offers two different services – virtual circuits and datagrams.

A *virtual circuit* is a 'logical connection' providing an error-free transmission of packets between terminals. A virtual circuit may be set up as a permanent connection or established for the duration of a call. (CCITT recommendations X25 packet protocol defines a permanent connection as a *permanent virtual circuit* and a temporary connection as a *virtual call*.) To set up a virtual circuit the terminal initiating the connection sends a call request packet which contains the addresses of both terminals. If the called terminal accepts the transmission it transmits a call accepted packet. Each virtual circuit is identified by a logical channel number. Once a circuit has been set up addresses need not be specified in the data packets as they can be determined from the logical channel number.

If a central supervisor calculates the route to be taken by packets then a unique channel number can be assigned to the circuit. If each node is responsible for calculating the link along which it will forward the packet then it is not possible for any one node to select a unique channel number for the entire route. Each node can only ensure that it assigns a unique logical channel number for the connection to the next node.

The route selected will remain fixed for the duration of the connection. Transmitting each packet along the same route ensures that the packets arrive in the correct sequence. If a packet is lost due to congestion or corruption then the network protocol will ensure that the packet is retransmitted. Lost packets can be detected very simply by using a single bit as a sequence indicator. The value of this bit alternates in each packet transmitted. If two consecutive packets arrive at the destination with the same sequence indicator value then a packet in between must have been lost. A sequence number allocated to each packet can be used to detect the loss of more than one packet. Each packet correctly received is acknowledged by the destination node.

A *datagram* is a self-contained packet transmitted without reference to any other packet. Every datagram packet carries both source and destination address. The network layer does not guarantee that a datagram will be delivered, or that the datagrams will arrive in the same sequence that they were transmitted. A datagram may be transmitted along any route through the network. Two consecutive datagrams between the same two terminals may follow different routes. The network layer protocol does not offer any error control; datagrams may be lost, duplicated or corrupted. The user is responsible for sequencing and error control.

Only terminals which have sufficient processing capability to assemble and disassemble messages into packets and vice versa may transmit and receive datagrams.

A virtual circuit can be established using an underlying datagram protocol with end-to-end error and sequence checking added.

Public carrier services

The public packet switching services support two classes of terminal – packet terminals and character terminals.

Packet terminals are sophisticated terminals capable of transmitting and receiving data as packets. The terminals assemble the data to be transmitted into packets and transmit them along leased lines to the packet switching exchange. The packet terminals, therefore, may use either the virtual circuit protocol or datagrams. The packet terminals operate in synchronous mode at speeds of between 2400 and 4800 bps. Packet terminals usually have their own processing capabilities and may establish several logical connections at the same time.

Character terminals, as the name implies, transmit one character at a time, generally at fairly low speeds (110 bps to 1200 bps). Transmission between the terminal and the packet switching exchange may be along leased lines or public telephone lines. Character terminals are not capable of assembling data into packets. The nodes to which the terminals are connected must have facilities for assembling character strings into packets and for disassembling packets into character strings. Character terminals cannot transmit or receive datagrams but must use the virtual circuit protocol.

The International Telegraph and Telephone Consultative Committee, more usually known by the initials CCITT, have laid down recommendations governing the connection of character terminals to a packet switching network. Recommendation X3 describes the functions of the PAD (packet assembler/disassembler). Recommendation X28 and X29 describe the interface and exchange of messages between the PAD and the character terminal.

The PAD receives streams of characters from the terminal which it assembles into packets. Similarly packets destined for the terminal are converted into streams of characters by the PAD. The PAD is also responsible for performing functions such as establishing and clearing a call.

Services

Most public packet switching services provide both datagram and virtual call facilities. The virtual calls may be set up as permanent links or established for the duration of a session of transmission.

Groups of users may form closed user groups. The users can communicate with each other but users outside the groups are not permitted access to the group. A user may be a member of more than one group.

Reverse charge call facilities are usually provided by public networks. This is an optional facility which enables a calling terminal to request a reversed charge call. When a user becomes a subscriber he must indicate whether he will accept reverse charge calls. The user retains the right to accept or reject particular requests. International reverse charge calls cannot usually be made or accepted.

Public networks are usually national rather than international. International services can be provided by interconnecting adjacent national networks. This interconnection between two networks is called a bridge or gateway. CCITT recommendation X75 describes the protocols governing the interconnection of networks. The X75 recommendation contains three levels, which describe the physical layer, the data link layer and the network layer. These protocols differ slightly from the corresponding X25 recommendations for public networks. The physical layer permits higher-speed links to be established. If the networks are not using the same protocols then the gateway will be responsible for any conversions necessary between the protocols.

The data link layer is designed to allow satellite links to be used. If a link is broken then the connection can be re-established by the node at either end of the gateway. The network layer only permits virtual calls which are established for the duration of the call.

Packet subaddressing can be used to identify a particular terminal in another network. The packet destination address field will contain the address of the network-to-network bridge (the interface between the two networks). The bridge may have to alter the packet format to conform to the destination network packet format. The destination and source addresses must be replaced by the subaddresses contained within the packet.

Exercises

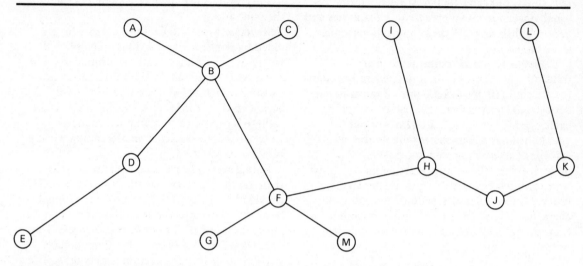

Figure 92   *Network for Exercise 9.1*

9.1 (a) The reliability of the network in Figure 92 could be improved by introducing further links. Select which links should be added to the network.

(b) What would be a suitable routing strategy for the redesigned network?

(c) How should the possibility of conges-tion be handled within the network?

9.2 What are the main functions of the network layer protocol?

9.3 What are the main functions of the data link layer protocol?

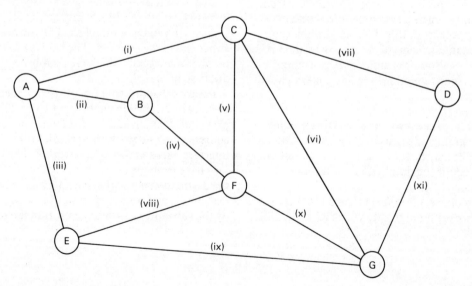

Figure 93   *Network for Exercise 9.5*

9.4 What is the difference between a virtual circuit and a datagram?

9.5 The time taken for a packet to be transmitted across each link in the network of Figure 93 is given by the following table:

(i)   A → C = 2.0 s   C → A = 2.0 s
(ii) A → B = 1.1 s   B → A = 1.1 s
(iii) A → E = 2.2 s   E → A = 2.1 s
(iv) B → F = 1.8 s   F → B = 1.6 s
(v)   C → F = 1.9 s   F → C = 1.9 s
(vi) C → G = 4.2 s   G → C = 3.8 s

(vii) C → D = 2.3 s   D → C = 2.3 s
(viii) E → F = 1.4 s   F → E = 1.4 s
(ix)   E → G = 2.8 s   G → E = 3.1 s
(x)   F → G = 1.9 s   G → F = 2.1 s
(xi)   D → G = 2.1 s   G → G = 2.0 s

The times given for each link take into account the delay at each node while a packet waits for transmission. Calculate the routing table for node G in a network using Delta routing. (Assume Delta = 0·5 seconds.)

10   Local area networks

Computing power has been gradually moving away from the computer room and into the office, first with the multi-access terminal and subsequently with the desk-top microcomputer. Microcomputers have proved remarkably successful owing to their low cost and the ease with which they can be used. The operating system of the microcomputer does not have to cope with the demands of several different users all with different requirements, but can instead be written with 'ease of use' as the most important design consideration. The microcomputer is, however, limited in its capabilities. It does not have the power to process many of the more demanding applications packages. File storage space tends to be limited; large backing stores would be expensive to provide and the air conditioning required would interfere with the normally quiet atmosphere of the office. The quality of peripherals associated with a microcomputer is usually fairly poor in comparison with those provided with mainframe computers. The cost of providing high-quality peripherals for every microcomputer would be prohibitive, but high-quality peripherals can be shared between several microcomputers using a local area network (LAN). Microcomputers, word processors, large mainframes and terminals can all be connected using a local area network. Stand-alone systems to access high-quality printers and large-volume backing stores can be added to this network. The provision of a large file storage system permits data relating to the whole organization to be centrally updated.

The characteristics of a local area network can be summarized as:

Covering a small geographic area; usually the network is housed within a single building or site
High-speed communications; faster than would normally be provided by telephone links
Sharing of centralized resources.

The local area networks can be classified according to their topology and the protocols used to transmit information.

The Cambridge Ring

Topology
The Cambridge Ring is a closed-loop network (Figure 94). It can be used to provide a terminal user with access to a mainframe or to provide a microcomputer user with facilities beyond the modest capabilities of his own microcomputer system. The Cambridge Ring can be used to connect a large number of dissimilar systems together.

Each node on the ring consists of a host, which may be a processor, server or terminal concentrator, a station, which is responsible for transmitting and receiving packets of data, and a repeater which is responsible for forwarding bit patterns from one node to the next (Figure 95).

The repeater
The stream of bits transmitted around the network is received by each repeater in turn. The repeater copies the bit pattern into the station's packet register. The station may change the bit pattern before returning it to the repeater, which forwards the bit pattern to the next repeater. A repeater takes its power from the ring, so that if a host computer is switched off the service is not disrupted. The distance between repeaters will depend upon the transmission medium used, but may be as much as 800 metres. There is no need for the same medium to be used for every connection. Coaxial cables, twisted pairs of copper wire, or optical fibres may be used as the transmission medium.

The station
The station is responsible for transmitting and receiving packets. Communication between the stations is actually in the form of minipackets. The station examines the bit streams received by

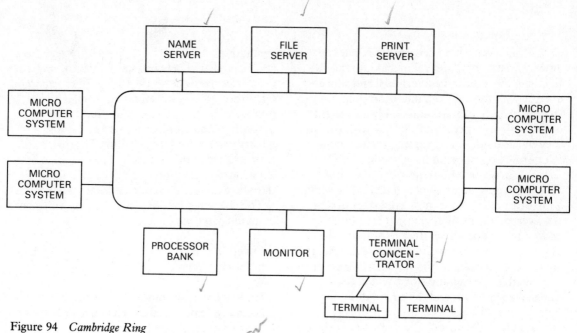

Figure 94   *Cambridge Ring*

HOST

STATION

REPEATER

Figure 95   *Node structure*

the repeater to identify minipackets destined for the station, and passes these packets to the host. If the host wishes to transmit data, the station examines the minipackets circulating through the ring until it finds an empty minipacket.

One station is special and has no host; this is the monitor. The functions of the monitor are to start up the ring and to prevent the propagation of errors. The monitor also provides power to the ring which is used to power the repeater stations. The other stations are powered by the hosts and not by the ring. Whether a station is switched on or off has no effect upon the integrity of the ring.

Processors

A microcomputer has modest processing capabilities. When a user wishes to perform processing that is beyond the capabilities of his machine, then he may request access to a more powerful processor from the processor bank.

The processor bank is controlled by a resource manager. The user specifies the type of processor required and the software to be used. The resource manager will check that the user is entitled to make such a request before determining whether sufficient resources are available to meet the request.

A microcomputer system may have its own localized storage system and printer terminal, but processors from the processor bank make use of the file server and print server.

Servers

One of the objectives of a local area network is to provide users with access to resources not provided by their own microcomputer system or terminal. In a Cambridge Ring network these facilities are provided by servers. There is no central scheduling policy controlling access to the servers; each user is responsible for his own control. If a user attempts to access a server which is temporarily unavailable, it is the user's responsibility to try again later.

The more commonly provided services include:

Name server   The topology of a network is likely to change dynamically as services are added to and deleted from the ring. Rather than inform all stations of changes to the ring, the identity of all stations currently connected to the ring are held in the name server.

File server   The file server is a centralized filing system which provides the user with access to a large-volume backing store and which controls the allocation of file space, access to files and file security.

Print server   High-quality printed output can be obtained using the print server.

Terminal concentrators

A terminal concentrator can be used to connect up to sixteen terminals, or microcomputers operating as terminals, to the ring. The terminal concentrator organizes the connection of the user's terminal to one of the processors or servers. Once the control program within the terminal concentrator has established contact between the terminal and another host, then it acts as a channel through which data passes to and from the terminal. Data passing between the terminal and the terminal concentrator can be buffered by the concentrator and built up into records. The contents of the buffer can be altered by the user before it is forwarded to the appropriate processor or server. Alternatively the concentrator can operate in 'transparent' mode where every key stroke by the user results in a character being sent directly to the appropriate host.

Packet protocols

Two packet protocols are used: the single shot protocol, which consists of a simple request and reply sequence, and the byte stream protocol, which permits a 'virtual channel' to be established between any two stations.

The single shot protocol is used by many of the less sophisticated server stations. Where more sophisticated transmission is required, then the byte stream protocol is used. The byte stream protocol permits hosts to conduct a bidirectional dialogue. The byte stream protocol uses a sequence number in each packet to ensure that no packets are lost or duplicated.

Packet formats

A packet is usually transmitted as a number of minipackets in the sequence

> Header minipacket
> Route minipacket
> 1–1024 data minipackets
> Checksum minipacket.

Header minipacket

A four-bit pattern (1001) indicates that this is a header packet; the next two bits are used to indicate the packet type. Packet types are as follows:

00	packet conforming to above sequence including checksum
01	packet conforming to above sequence excluding checksum (a little-used option provided for stations which cannot compute the checksum)
10	packet consists of a single minipacket in which the ten remaining bits carry the data.

The remaining ten bits will normally define the number of data minipackets following.

Route minipacket

A twelve-bit field defines the logical port within a station. The host may be a terminal concentrator to which are connected several microcomputers. The port number would indicate which microcomputer is being addressed. The remaining four bits can be used to carry information on the type of packet for higher levels of software.

Data minipackets

Up to 1024 data packets can follow the header and route minipackets carrying 2048 bytes of data.

Checksum minipacket

The host minipacket will contain the checksum. This is calculated using 16-bit carry-around

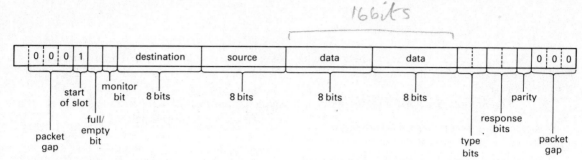

Figure 96   *Minipacket format*

addition on the contents of the header, route and data minipackets. If the packet type is 01, the checksum value will be zero.

Transmission of packets
The Cambridge Ring uses an empty slot protocol (isarithmic control). A small number of minipackets circulate continually around the ring. The number of minipackets circulating is determined by the length of the connections and the number of repeaters (typically only two or three). Any station wishing to transmit waits until it detects an empty minipacket. The station loads the minipacket with its own data and forwards it around the ring. If the destination station is in a position to receive the minipacket it will copy the packet contents into its own register, mark the packet as received and return the minipacket to the transmitting station. The transmitting station will check the contents of the minipacket upon its return, to verify that the data has not been corrupted during transmission. The station will then mark the minipacket as empty and return it to the ring.

The minipacket format is shown in Figure 96. The start-of-slot marker heralds the start of another minipacket. This has the value 1 to distinguish it from the interpacket gap, which is all zeros.

The full/empty bit is used to indicate whether the packet is in use (full = 1, empty = 0). The transmitting station will load the source and destination addresses into the packet as well as the sixteen data bits. The response bits are set to 11, and the parity bit is adjusted before the packet is forwarded round the ring.

The monitor bit is initally set to 1 by the transmitting station. When the monitor detects a packet it will check the packet for errors. If no

errors are detected by the monitor, the monitor bit is changed to zero and the parity bit inverted accordingly. If the monitor should detect any irregularities, then the monitor bit remains unaltered but the full/empty marker is set to empty.

If two stations are engaged in a dialogue then they may wish to receive packets only from each other. For example, a print server can only output results from one user at a time. No other user should be permitted to access the print server at the same time. The receiving station must be able to identify the station from which it is receiving packets and only accept packets from that station. Each station has a unique one-byte identifier which is used as its address. If one station is engaged in a dialogue with another then it holds the address of the other station in a special register called the source acquisition register (SAR). The source acquisition register can be set to accept packets from

Any other station (SAR = 255)
A particular station (SAR = address of station)
No other station (SAR = 0).

When a station receives a minipacket with its own address in the destination bits, it compares the source address with the contents of the source acquisition register. The response bits of the minipacket are set as a result of this comparison. If the receiving station is not set to receive from the station that transmitted the minipacket then the response bits are set to 10, which indicates to the transmitting station that the packet has been rejected.

A station may not be able to accept a minipacket because its reception register (into which the minipacket would be placed) is already full. In this case the minipacket response bits are set to 00 (busy) and the minipacket is returned. If the minipacket is accepted then the minipacket contents will be copied into the station reception register, the response bits are set to 01 (accepted) and the packet is returned to the transmitting station.

If the station for which the packet is destined is switched off then the minipacket will return to the transmitting station with its response bit still set to 11 (initial value – passed by all stations).

Ethernet

The Ethernet design was developed by Xerox (office equipment) at their Palo Alto Research Centre. Ethernet is based on a two-way bus topology to which a large variety of devices may be connected. Control is wholly distributed among the work stations. Each work station is responsible for controlling its own transmission of packets, which may be broadcast along the bus at any time.

The packet header will contain the source and destination addresses of the packet and, although the packet will be received by all the other stations, only the destination for which it is intended will respond. Ethernet uses a collision detection mechanism to ensure that no two stations transmit packets simultaneously. The full name for this technique is carrier sense multiple access with collision detection (CSMA-CD).

Topology
In Ethernet terminology, the two-way bus along which packets are transmitted is called the ether. The ether is named after the medium through which electromagnetic waves were supposed to have been transmitted. The ether may be implemented using twisted pairs of copper wires (as for telephone wiring) or coaxial cable (as for television aerials). Fibre optic cables offer great potential for the future, but the necessary T-junction connections are not yet available.

Every station is connected to the ether by a tap and a transceiver (Figure 97). The physical

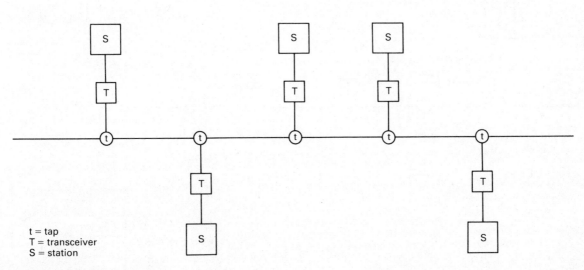

t = tap
T = transceiver
S = station

Figure 97   *Ethernet topology*

connection between the station and the ether is made by the tap. The tap connection must be designed in such a way that it disturbs the transmissions along the ether as little as possible. The transceiver is responsible for transmitting packets and for monitoring all packets received. Packets destined for a station are detected by the transceiver and copied into the station's memory.

One of the most important aspects of transceiver design is that, no matter what faults might occur, the transceiver must not be allowed to interfere with the ether. The network may assume a tree structure as several ethers may be connected together (Figure 98). Packets in one ether segment will be copied into interconnecting ether segments by the repeater stations. The ether segments can be connected in any pattern providing that no closed loops are formed; to do so would mean that two copies of a packet could arrive at the destination station. If a repeater fails then one or more segments may be isolated. However, the network is not dead; it merely functions as two distinct partial networks.

The branch lines of the network which are formed by the interconnecting segments permit the network to follow the physical layout of the installation in which it is housed.

As the taps cause minimal interference to the

ether, it is possible to add work stations at any point, subject to an overall maximum number of work stations for the network. The maximum number of work stations is defined by the address portion of each packet. An 8-bit address will allow up to 256 stations to be uniquely identified. The addressing can be extended by using a single address to represent the gateway to another network or a collective address for a multiport station. Further fields within the packet can then be used to identify the appropriate source or destination point.

Packet transmission
Ethernet exercises no central control over the transmission of packets, which means that each work station is free to transmit at any time it finds the network is unused. In a system that allows stations to transmit at will it is quite probably that two stations will attempt to transmit simultaneously. Packets transmitted at the same time are said to collide. To avoid the collision of packets, all stations continuously sense the ether for other stations transmitting. No station will transmit if it detects that another station is already doing so.

Although transmission through the network is fast, it will still take time for the packets to be

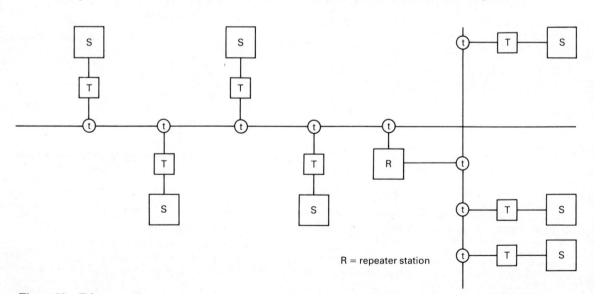

R = repeater station

Figure 98   *Ethernet treeing*

propagated through the network. It is during this time that another station may start to transmit and cause a collision. As soon as a station senses that another station is also transmitting, it will immediately cease transmitting. The transmitting station that detects a collision will transmit a jamming signal. It will transmit this signal long enough to ensure that all other transmitting station realize that a collision has occured. To avoid the possibility of repeated collisions, both stations will wait for a random interval before attempting to retransmit.

If repeated collisions do occur then the transmitting station will wait for increasingly longer periods. Once a station has been transmitting long enough for the first bits transmitted to have reached all other stations, it will be free to complete the transmission.

A station that attempts to transmit, but finds the network in use, is deferred. If two stations are deferred during the transmission of the same packet then a collision is quite likely to occur, as both stations will start to transmit as soon as the network becomes free.

Token passing

The Cambridge Ring and Ethernet illustrate two common topologies used in local area networks. They also demonstrate two of the more common access techniques – empty slot, and carrier sense multiple access with collision detection. One other common access technique is token passing.

The token passing protocol is based upon the principle of a token that passes from station to station. Whichever station is in possession of the token is free to transmit. The token is a unique bit pattern that must not be allowed to occur within the data. Stations are usually restricted to transmitting only one packet before passing the token on. This avoids the possibility that one station will monopolize the network. IBM's local area network uses a token passing access protocol.

Local area networks and satellite links

One of the restrictions upon local area networks which is inherent in the very concept of a localized network is that the network is confined to a small geographic area. Experiments are currently taking place to determine the feasibility of connecting local area networks through satellite links. One of these experiments is project UNIVERSE which is being undertaken by British Telecom and research laboratories in universities and industry.

Exercises

10.1 What are the important characteristics of a local area network?

10.2 Which of the topologies described in Chapter 9 would be suitable for a local area network?

10.3 If your college's microcomputers are already linked by a local area network, find out (a) what is the network topology (b) what packet protocol is used.

or
If your college's microcomputers are not connected to a local area network, design a suitable network topology to link the microcomputers in your college and select an appropriate packet protocol.

Outline solutions to exercises

Chapter 2

2.1

Command Languages	*Job control languages*
Function based	Job based
User friendly	Often require specialist knowledge of the computer system
Similar repertoire of commands in all systems	Non-portable

For further details the reader is referred to the sections on job control languages and command languages within this chapter.

2.2

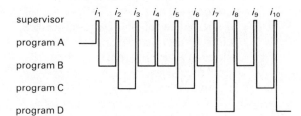

2.3 The program execution sequence will be

$$D C D C D B A C D$$

At the end of the 9 second period lists 1 and 2 will both be empty. List 3 will be as follows

List 3
B(2)
A(3)
C(1)
D(1)

Chapter 3

3.1 In a multiprogramming environment each program will be allocated short periods of CPU time. During each of these periods only a relatively few instructions will be executed. Instructions and data areas not referred to will occupy unnecessary storage space. If programs in store have to be swapped with programs on backing store then copying entire programs is inefficient.

3.2 (a) When a program is loaded it is not necessarily possible to determine whether the contents of a storage location represents an instruction or data. The base value of the programs should only be added to operand addresses.
(b) The number of bits within an instruction used to represent operand addresses is not usually sufficient to represent all actual memory addresses.

3.3 Segmentation is the division of the program into logically distinct sections of code which may be of various sizes, while paging is the division of the program into physically equal sections of code.

3.4 (a) By adding the base register value to the program addresses.
(b) To ensure that locations accessed by the program lie within the program's own area of store.
(c) First-fit
1 Program E placed in slot (i)

2 Program F placed in slot (ii)
3 Program G placed in slot (iv)
4 Program H remains in job queue
5 Program D releases 8K of store giving a single contiguous area of store from address locations 78K to 90K, not large enough to accommodate program H

Best-fit

1 Program E placed in slot (ii)
2 Program F placed in slot (iii)
3 Program G placed in slot (i)
4 Program H remains in job queue
5 Program D releases 8K of store adjacent to slot (iv). This single area of store is large enough to accommodate program H

Worst-fit

1 Program E placed in slot (iv)
2 Program F placed in slot (i)
3 Program G remains in job queue
4 Program H remains in job queue
5 Program D releases area of store which is combined with slot (iii), program G can be loaded into this area

3.5 When the use bit values are taken in account the user register contents become

Page frame

0	1	2	3	4	5	6	7	8	9	10	11	12	13	14	15

Register values

1011 1100 0001 1111 0001 1111 1010 0001 1001 0011 1110 0000 0010 1101 1110 0110

(a) The page selected from program X would be page X4 held in page frame number 11.
(b) The page selected from program Y would be page Y3 held in page frame number 4.
Page Y7 has an identical use register value but its write bit is set indicating that the contents of the page have been altered.
(c) The page selected from program Z would be page Z6 held in page frame number 15.

Page Z2 has a lower use register value but will not be selected as its write bit is set.

The following pages would be selected if a least-frequently-used policy were used

(a) Progam X   page X4
(b) Program Y   page Y7
(c) Program Z   page Z6

3.6 (a) Virtual peripherals are peripherals which do not actually exist but which are simulated on another device. In this way it is possible to emulate several printers on a magnetic disk drive in an installation with only one physical printer.
(b) Shared peripherals are devices which may be allocated to more than one program at the same time, such as a magnetic disk.
(c) Dedicated peripherals are peripherals which by their nature can only be allocated to one program at a time. All serial access devices such as printers fall into this category.
Any number of virtual peripherals may be allocated. The device management system does not have to determine whether a peripheral of the desired type is available. A shared peripheral may be allocated to several different programs. A dedicated peripheral of the correct type must be available before it can be allocated.

3.7 Device identifier
Device control unit identifier
Operation required
Direction of transfer
Store addresses

Disk address
Amount of data to be transferred
Reply word

3.8 A read or write statement does not always result in a peripheral transfer because the unit of data transferred between the device and the processor is dependent upon the characteristics of the device and not the program's input/output statements. If a program is reading records from a disk file then the unit of transfer will be a block of data that may well contain several records. One peripheral transfer will result in several records being transferred into store. Each time a program read statement is encountered one of these records will be moved into the program's buffer. Only when all the records have been processed will another peripheral transfer take place.

3.9 Storage lockout is used to prevent
(a) Storage locations involved in read instructions from being accessed before the data has arrived.
(b) Storage locations involved in write instructions from being altered before the data has been output.

3.10 Storage lockout for a write statement need not prevent other statements from accessing locations within the locked out area providing these statements do not alter the contents of any of these locations. A read statement will alter the contents of some or all of the locations locked out and all other accesses must be prevented until the data values have been input.

Chapter 4

4.1 To provide a simple mechanism for creating and accessing files.
To provide a facility for editing the contents of a file.
To protect files against unauthorized access.
To protect files from hardware or software malfunction.

4.2 The reader is referred to the sections on the identification of files and control of access.

4.3 (a) /USER0/USER1/USER3.FILE3B
or
..USER4..USER1/USER3.FILE3B
(b) /USER0/USER2/USER5.FILEZ

4.4 (a) The owner – write status
Privileged users – write status
General users – no access
(b) The owner – write status
Privileged users – write status
General users – no access
(c) The owner – write status
Privileged users – execute only
General users – execute only
(d) The owner – write status
Privileged users – write status
General users – write status

Chapter 5

5.1 A compiler produces an object code program which can be saved and subsequently loaded and executed. An interpreter translates the source program into an internal version and then simulates the execution of the program. For a more detailed description of compilers and interpreters the reader is referred to the text of this chapter.

5.2 An incremental compiler does not process complete programs but processes each line as it is input. All other types of compiler consider each source line in the context of the preceding and succeeding lines of text.

5.3 In a multipass compiler each of the stages of translation are performed by a separate routine which takes as input either the original source program or the output from the previous routine. Each stage of the translation process is completed before the next stage is started. A single pass compiler performs all of the stages of translation on each statement in turn.

5.4 A true single pass compiler is not possible if the program is to be allowed to contain forward branches.

5.5 The purpose of the lexical analysis routine is to convert the elements of the source program into symbols acceptable to the subsequent stages of the compiler. The reader is referred to the section on lexical analysis for further details of the functions of the lexical analyser.

5.6 (a) Parse tree for
$$Y := A * X ** 2 + B * X + C$$

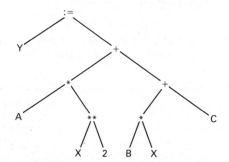

Triple sequence

Triple no.		Triple		
(i)	*	,	B	, X
(ii)	+	,	(i)	, C
(iii)	**	,	X	, 2
(iv)	*	,	A	, (iii)
(v)	+	,	(iv)	, (ii)
(vi)	:=	,	Y	, (v)

(b) Parse tree for VOL := PI * R ** 2 * H

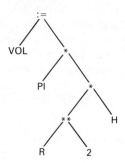

Triple sequence

Triple no.		Triple		
(i)	**	,	R	, 2
(ii)	*	,	(i)	, H
(iii)	*	,	PI	, (ii)
(iv)	:=	,	VOL	, (iii)

5.8 Within the inner loop the expression PI *(R ** 2)/3 is constant and can be removed to the outer loop. The strength of the exponentiation can be reduced to multiplication.

```
PI := 3.1415926;
FOR R := 1 TO 10 DO
BEGIN
        t1 := PI *(R * R)/3;
        FOR H := 1 TO 5 DO
                VOL [R, H] := t1 * H;
END;
```

The expression PI/3 can be evaluated at compile time. The inner loop can be unrolled.

```
FOR R := 1 TO 10 DO
BEGIN
      t1 := 1.0471975 * R * R;
      VOL [R,1] := t1 * 1;
      VOL [R,2] :- t1 * 2;
      VOL [R,3] :- t1 * 3;
      VOL [R,4] := t1 * 4;
      VOL [R,5] := t1 * 5;
END;
```

Each of the calculations within the inner loop represent a constant increment

i.e. VOL[R,2] := VOL[R,1] + t1;

The strength of the calculation can be reduced by holding the values calculated in a register and incrementing by t1.

Chapter 6

6.1 The advantages of using a database can be summarized as

A centralized approach to the storage of data
Data representation is independent of physical storage
Minimal redundancy in the storage of data
Improved data consistency
The user is shielded from changes made to the structure of the data
Reduces program development time and costs.

6.2 The principal stages in creating a database are

(a) Analyse the data and create the database definition file. The formal specification of the data is known as the schema and is defined using the data description language.

(b) The contents of the database definition file are input to the database description processor, which creates a description of the database in a form which the database management system can interpret.

(c) From the database description the database itself can be created. The empty database is created by the database processor.

6.3 The reader is referred to the section on the physical view of the database.

6.4 A data dictionary provides information about the data held within a database and it records descriptions of individual data fields, subschemas and schemas, the relationship between items of data and which processes use items of data. It can also be used to ensure that the contents of the database remain consistent and contain the minimum of redundant data items.

6.5 If two users simultaneously access the same record then the possibility exists that both users will fetch a copy of the record, update it and return it. The sequence of events is such that one of the updates could be lost if a system of update locks is not used. The reader is referred to the section on concurrency for further details.

6.6 (a) Sequential file of employee numbers and names:

EMPLOYEE NUMBER	NAME
01113	BLACK
01124	JOHNSON
01145	WHITE
01365	WILSON
01415	BROWN
01728	CAMPBELL
01837	GREEN
02161	JONES
02248	HOWARD

03141	SMITH
11234	JACKSON
11238	CARTER
11347	TAYLOR
12634	GORDON
21658	DAVIES

Inverted files for department, job title and sex:

DEPARTMENT

BUS STUDIES	03141, 02248, 21658, 12634, 11347
MATHEMATICS	02161, 01837, 01113, 01728, 11238
SCIENCE	01365, 01415, 01145, 01124, 11234

JOB TITLE

HEAD	03141, 01145, 01728
SECRETARY	01365, 01113, 12634
LECTURER	02161, 01837, 01124, 11234, 02248, 21658, 11347
TECHNICIAN	01415, 11238

SEX

M	03141, 01415, 01837, 01124, 11234, 02248, 11347
F	02161, 01365, 01113, 01145, 21658, 01728, 12634, 11238

(b)

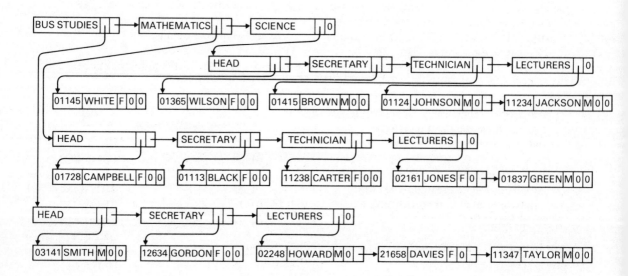

Chapter 7

7.1   (a)   TROPHIES database

Trophy#	Racecourse	Date	Time	WH/F	Distance
DB HANDICAP	CHEPSTOW	30/4	2.00	NH	3 miles
RELATIONAL STAKES	CHEPSTOW	30/4	2.30	F	2 miles
DATA CUP	NEWMARKET	16/5	2.15	F	1 mile

EQUINE database

Horse#	Owner	Horse-trainer
BAG OF BEANS	KERMIT	MISS PIGGY
GLAD RAGS	HERMIT	HOBO
DOBBIN	UGLY SISTERS	BUTTONS
TRIGGER	ROY ROGERS	ANNIE OAKLEY
CLOTHES	WISHEY WASHEY	MRS MOP
VAULTING	WALTER	JIM
POMMEL	HANS	JIM
EEYORE	A A MILNE	PIGLET
HOBBY	RED KITE	PEREGRINE

TRAINERS database

Racehorse-trainer#	Stable
MISS PIGGY	MUPPET SHOW
HOBO	PARK BENCH
BUTTONS	CASTLE STABLES
ANNIE OAKLEY	HOLLY WOOD
MRS MOP	LAUNDRY
JIM	NASIUM
PIGLET	THE WOLERY
PEREGRINE	THE EYRIE

RACE database

Race-trophy#	Racehorse#	Jockey	Weight	Odds
DB HANDICAP	BAG OF BEANS	FOZZY BEAR	10st 10lb	10–1
DB HANDICAP	GLAD RAGS	A TRAMP	9st 6lb	50–1
DB HANDICAP	DOBBIN	PRINCE CHARMING	8st 12lb	8–1
RELATIONAL STAKES	TRIGGER	R ROGERS	8st 7lb	EVENS
RELATIONAL STAKES	CLOTHES	MR BUN THE BAKER	8st 7lb	100–30

RELATIONAL STAKES	VAULTING	A LEAPER	8st 7lb	10–1
RELATIONAL STAKES	POMMEL	W JUMPER	8st 2lb	2–1
DATA CUP	EEYORE	CHRISTOPHER ROBIN	9st 00lb	3–1
DATA CUP	HOBBY	MERLIN	9st 00lb	EVENS

(b) There are many queries that could be made of the database, among the more likely are

Who is the owner of a particular horse?
Who trains a particular horse?
Where is the horse trained?
Who will be riding a particular horse in a particular event?
What will the odds be?
What weight will they be carrying?

(c) The primary key fields are all marked with a hash symbol (#) in the answer to part (a) of this question.
Indexes could be usefully added to the OWNER, TRAINER and JOCKEY fields in order to speed up the responses to queries such as
Find all horses owned by a particular owner.
Find all horses trained by a particular trainer.
Find all horses to be ridden by a particular jockey.

(d) FIND EQUINE
    WHERE HORSE = "GLAD RAGS"
FIND TRAINERS
    WHERE RACEHORSE-TRAINER = EQUINE-HORSE-TRAINER
SHOW TRAINERS.STABLE
FIND RACE
    WHERE (RACE-TROPHY = "DB HANDICAP")
    AND (RACE-HORSE = "GLAD RAGS")
SHOW RACE.JOCKEY

7.2 (a) Physical database record for hierarchical database.

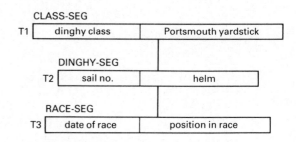

(b) ACCESS = HIDAM or ACCESS = HISAM would be equally suitable for such a straightforward structure.

(c)

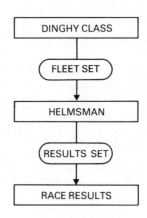

(d) The helmsman and race results should both be LINKED to OWNER in order to satisfy enquiries such as 'Who ran a particular race?' or 'What class of dinghy does a helmsman sail?'.
Forward pointers will be automatically provided.

7.3 A network approach would be most suitable.

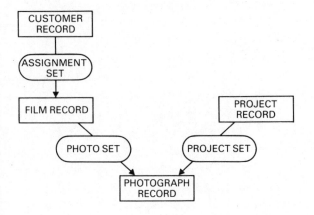

The CUSTOMER RECORD will record the customer name and assignment title.

The FILM RECORD will record the make, type and serial number of the film, the film speed and the development process used.

The PROJECT RECORD will record the subject of each personal project.

The PHOTOGRAPH RECORD will record where and when each photograph was taken, the aperture and shutter speed settings and the exposure time and filter settings used to print each photograph.

Chapter 8

8.1 Links
(a) Parallel, duplex, synchronous.
(b) Serial, duplex, synchronous.
(c) Serial, half duplex, asynchronous (depends upon the nature of the terminal – a keyboard-based terminal has been assumed).

8.2 The baud rate measures the number of 'signal' changes per second. In the simplest case a signal represents a single bit but the signal may represent two or three data bits.

8.3 The reader is referred to the sections on multiplexing and concentrators in answer to this question.

8.4 (a) Echo printing.
(b) Simplified error detection such as parity checking allied with resubmission of erroneous data.
(c) Use an error detection code and retransmission.
(d) Use an error detection code such as cyclic redundancy checking and retransmit all blocks of data containing errors.
(e) Use an error correcting code as the data transmitted will not be available for subsequent retransmission.

Chapter 9

9.1 (a)

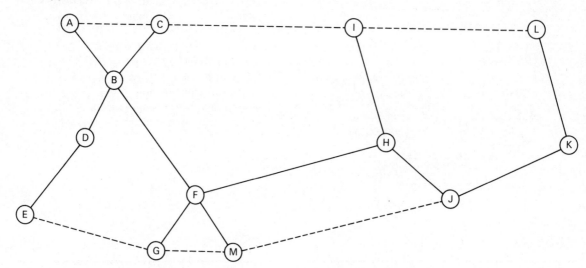

The criteria for the introduction of further links is to reduce the effect caused by the failure of a single node or line. Each node should be connected to at least two other nodes. Several different solutions exist which satisfy this requirement.

(b) A fixed alternative routing algorithm would be suitable as the network is so small.

(c) If no centralized supervisory control exists then any data arriving after the buffers have been filled will have to be discarded. The data link control must ensure that any discarded blocks of data are retransmitted.

9.2 The purpose of the network layer protocol is
(a) To select the routes for packets.
(b) To prevent congestion.
(c) To ensure that packets arrive in sequence.

9.3 The purpose of the data link protocol is primarily to ensure an error free transmission of blocks of data between nodes.

9.4 The reader is referred to the section on virtual circuits and datagrams in answer to this question.

9.5

Node to be reached	Link (vi)	(ix)	(x)	(xi)	Optimum link	Equivalent links (Delta = 0.5 s)
A	6.2 s	5.2 s	4.8 s	6.3 s	(x)	(ix)
B	7.3 s	6.1 s	3.7 s	7.4 s	(x)	
C	4.2 s	6.4 s	4.0 s	4.3 s	(x)	(vi) and (xi)
D	6.5 s	8.7 s	6.3 s	2.0 s	(xi)	
E	7.5 s	3.1 s	3.5 s	7.6 s	(ix)	(x)
F	6.1 s	4.5 s	2.1 s	6.2 s	(x)	

Chapter 10

10.1 Important characteristics are
Small geographic area
High speed communications

Sharing of centralized resources

10.2 Ring or bus networks are most suitable.

Index